MARVEL SUPER HERO SQUAD

SQUADDIES FOREVER!

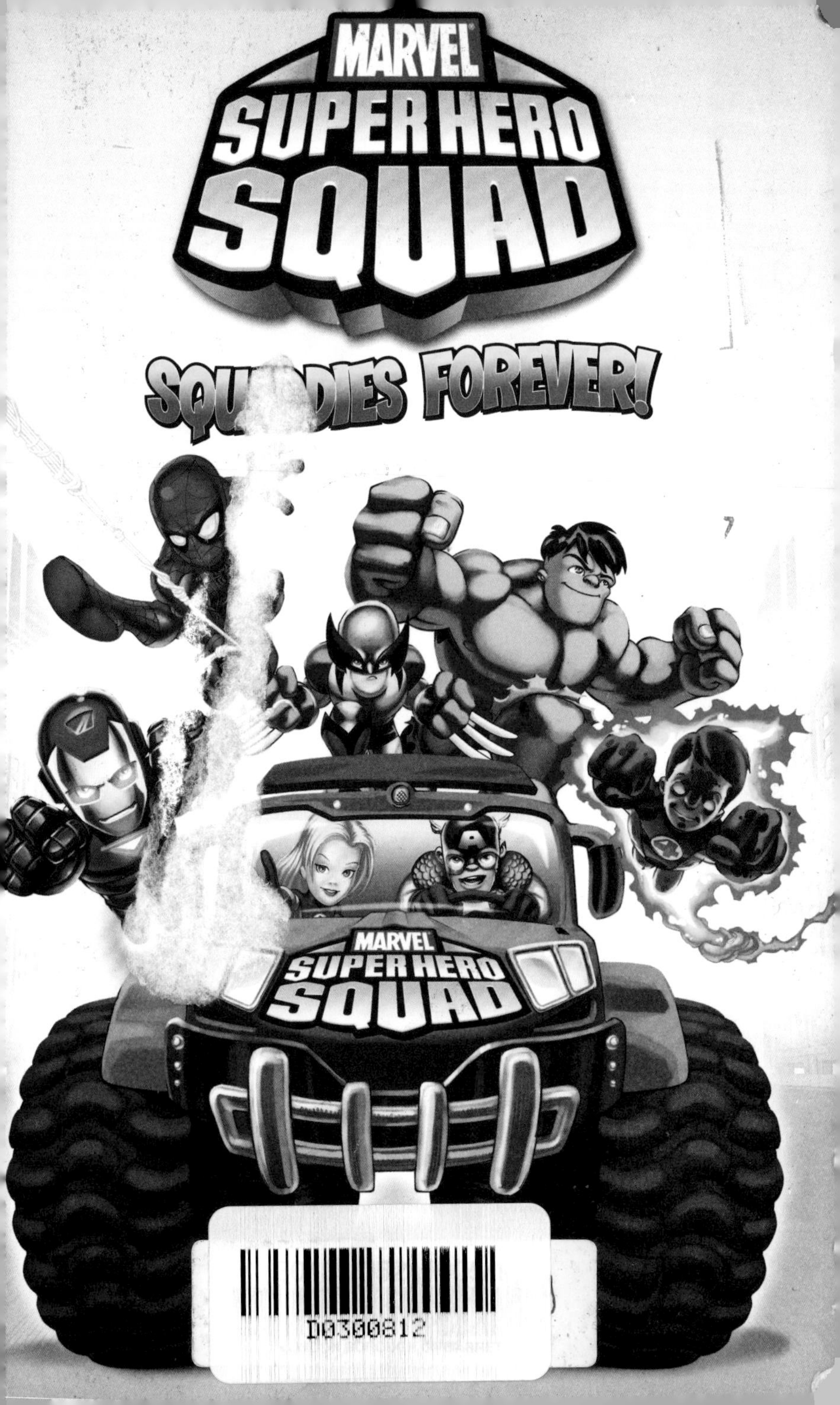
MARVEL
SUPER HERO
SQUAD

MARVEL SUPER HERO SQUAD

SQUADDIES FOREVER!

WRITERS: PAUL TOBIN & TODD DEZAGO

ARTISTS: DARIO BRIZUELA, LEONEL CASTELLANI & MARCELO DICHIARA

COLORS (SUPER HERO SQUAD #1-2): SOTOCOLOR

LETTERER: DAVE SHARPE

ASSISTANT EDITOR: MICHAEL HORWITZ

EDITOR: NATHAN COSBY

SPECIAL THANKS TO COURTNEY LANE, KAT JONES, CHRIS FONDACARO & TOM MARVELLI

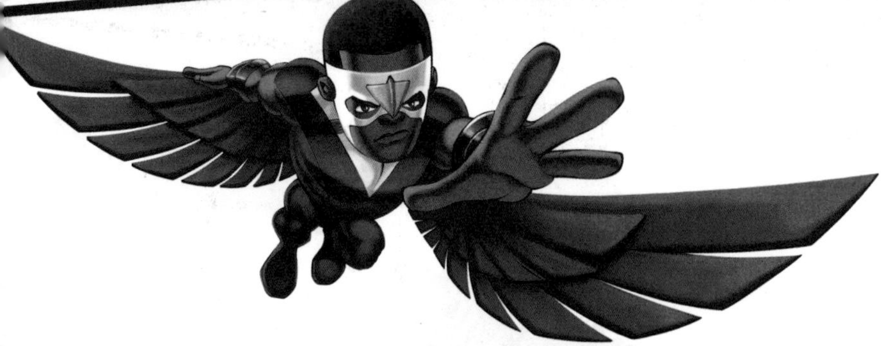

COLLECTION EDITOR: CORY LEVINE
EDITORIAL ASSISTANTS: JAMES EMMETT & JOE HOCHSTEIN
ASSISTANT EDITORS: ALEX STARBUCK & NELSON RIBEIRO
EDITORS, SPECIAL PROJECTS: JENNIFER GRÜNWALD & MARK D. BEAZLEY
SENIOR EDITOR, SPECIAL PROJECTS: JEFF YOUNGQUIST
SENIOR VICE PRESIDENT OF SALES: DAVID GABRIEL
BOOK DESIGN: PATRICK McGRATH

EDITOR IN CHIEF: JOE QUESADA
PUBLISHER: DAN BUCKLEY
EXECUTIVE PRODUCER: ALAN FINE

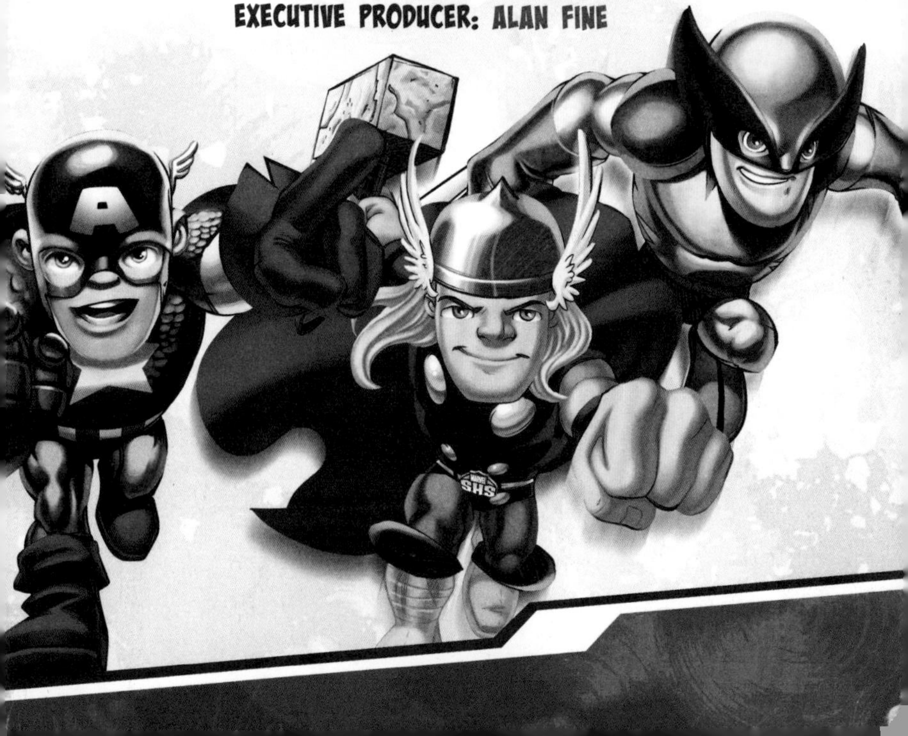
SHS

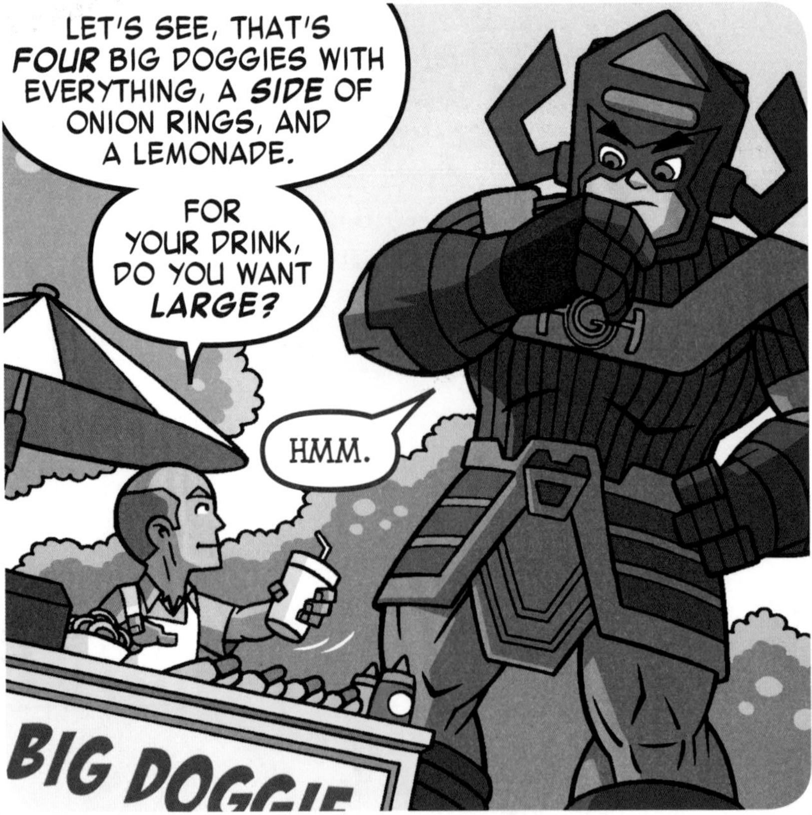
LET'S SEE, THAT'S FOUR BIG DOGGIES WITH EVERYTHING, A SIDE OF ONION RINGS, AND A LEMONADE.
FOR YOUR DRINK, DO YOU WANT LARGE?
HMM.
BIG DOGGIE

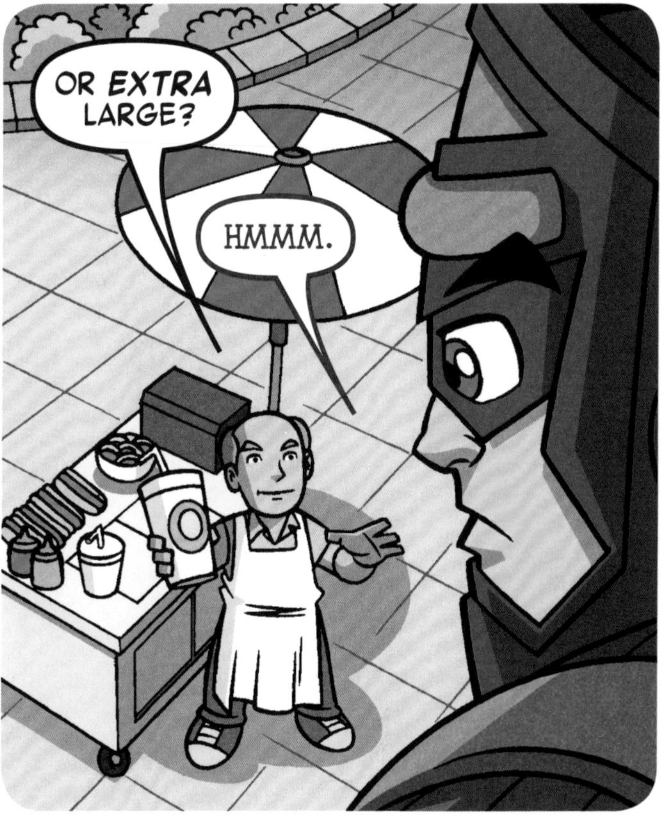
OR EXTRA LARGE?
HMMM.

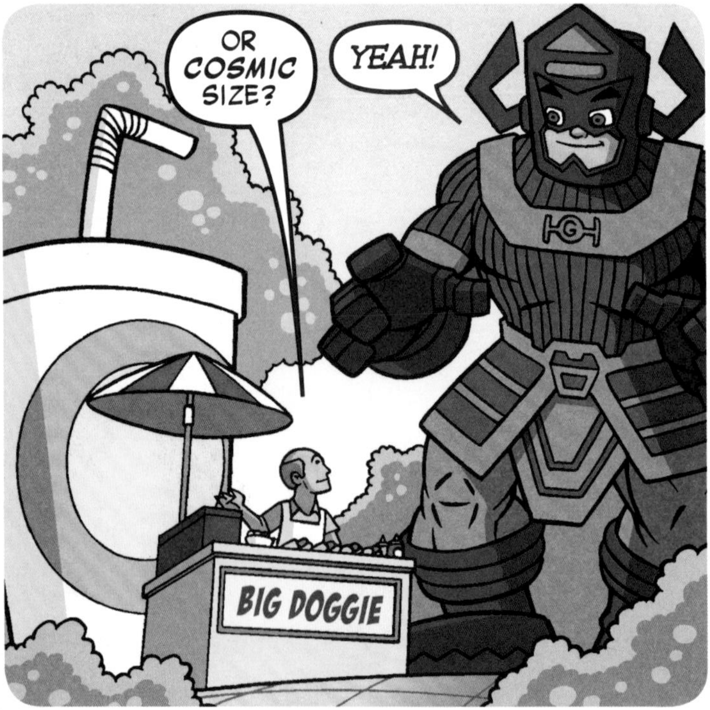
OR COSMIC SIZE?
YEAH!
BIG DOGGIE

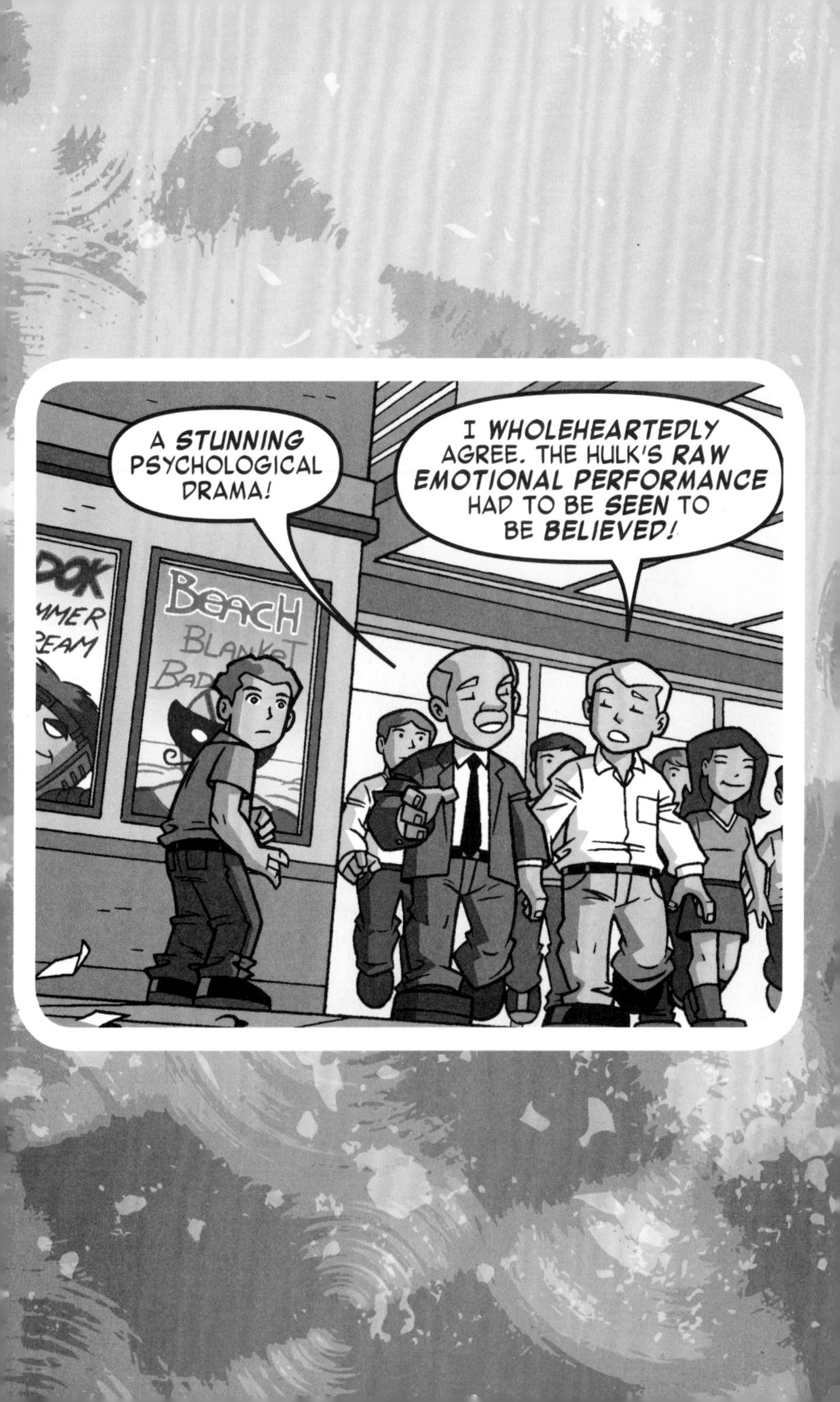
A *STUNNING* PSYCHOLOGICAL DRAMA!
I *WHOLEHEARTEDLY* AGREE. THE HULK'S *RAW EMOTIONAL PERFORMANCE* HAD TO BE *SEEN* TO BE *BELIEVED!*
BEACH BLANKET

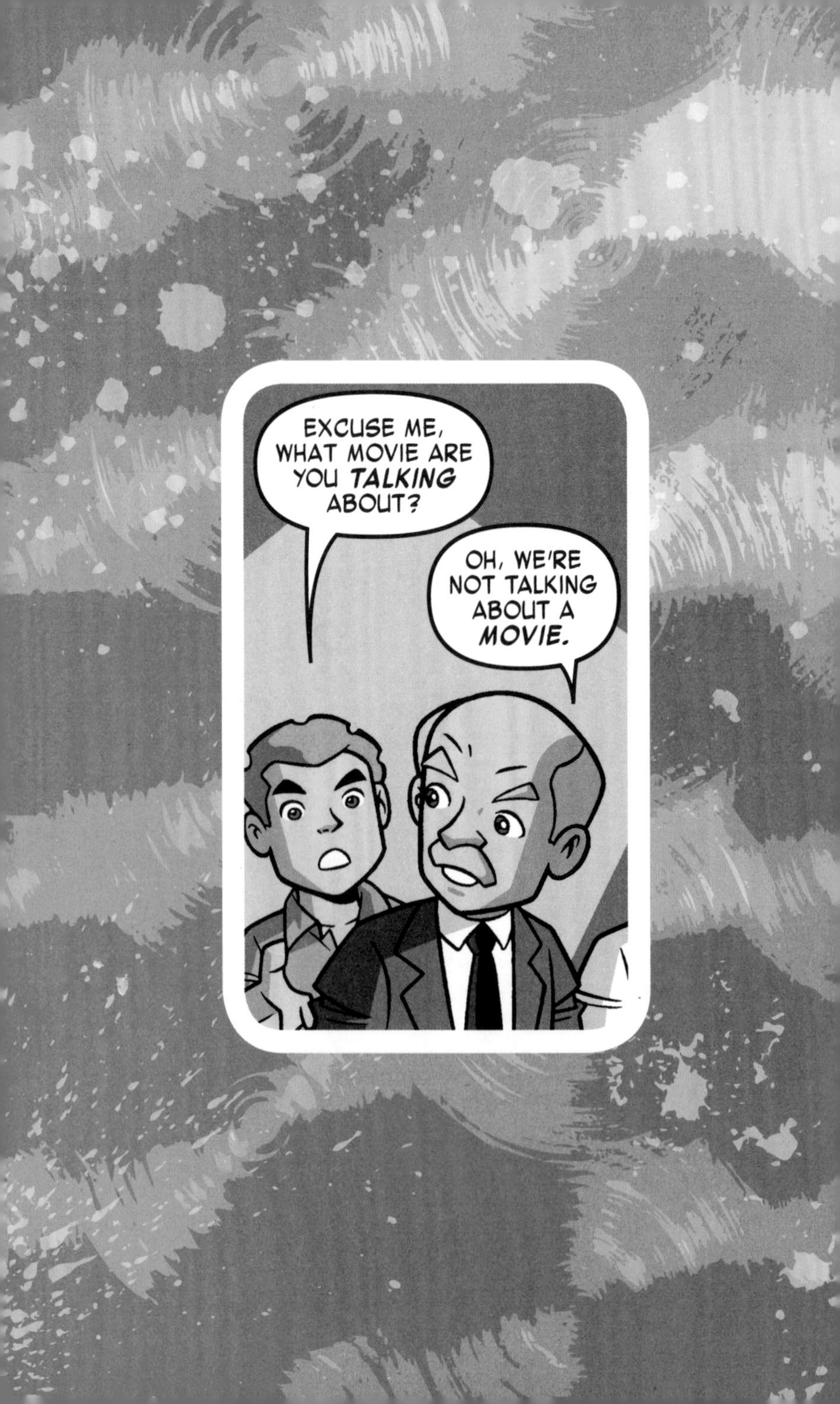
EXCUSE ME, WHAT MOVIE ARE YOU *TALKING* ABOUT?
OH, WE'RE NOT TALKING ABOUT A *MOVIE.*

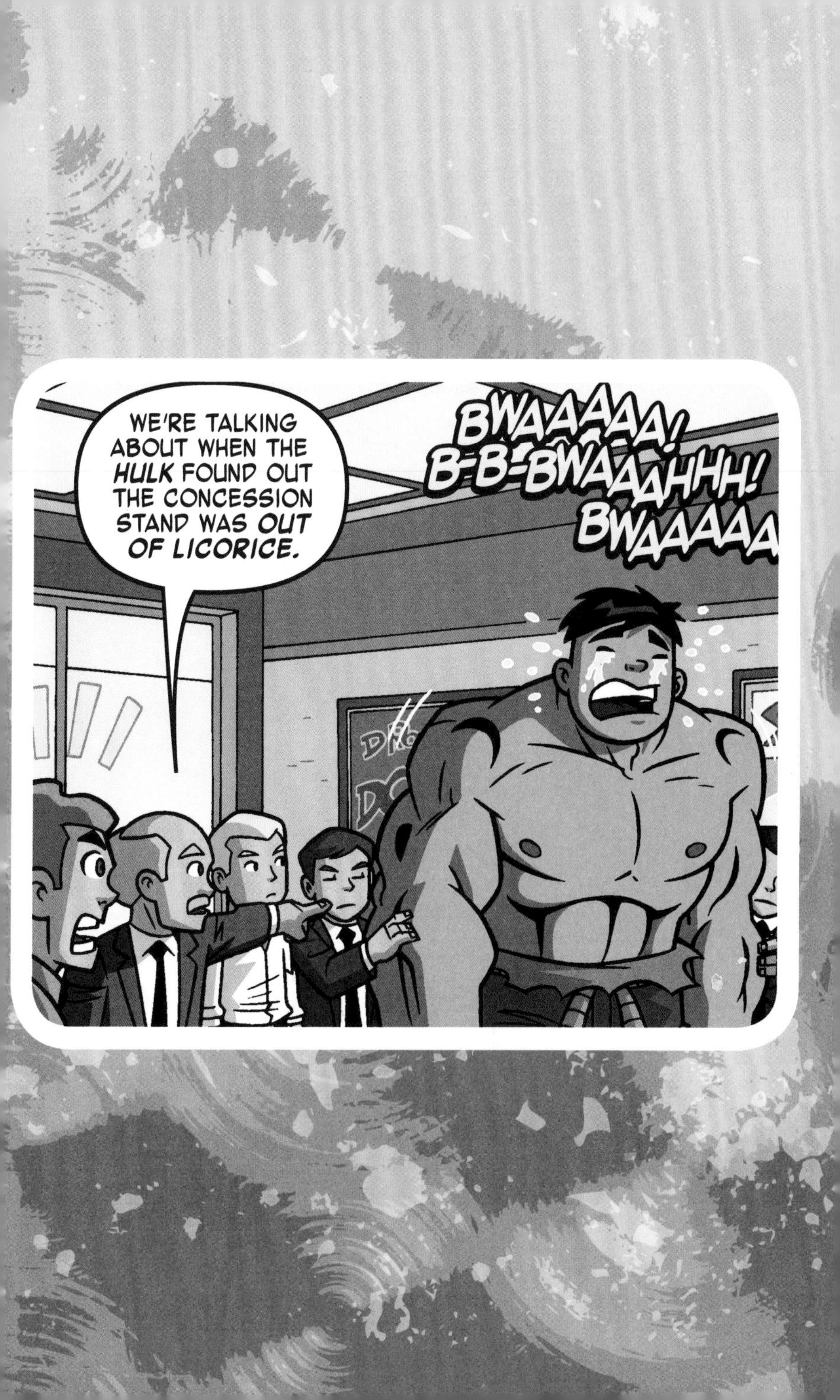
WE'RE TALKING ABOUT WHEN THE HULK FOUND OUT THE CONCESSION STAND WAS OUT OF LICORICE.
BWAAAAA! B-B-BWAAAHHH! BWAAAAA

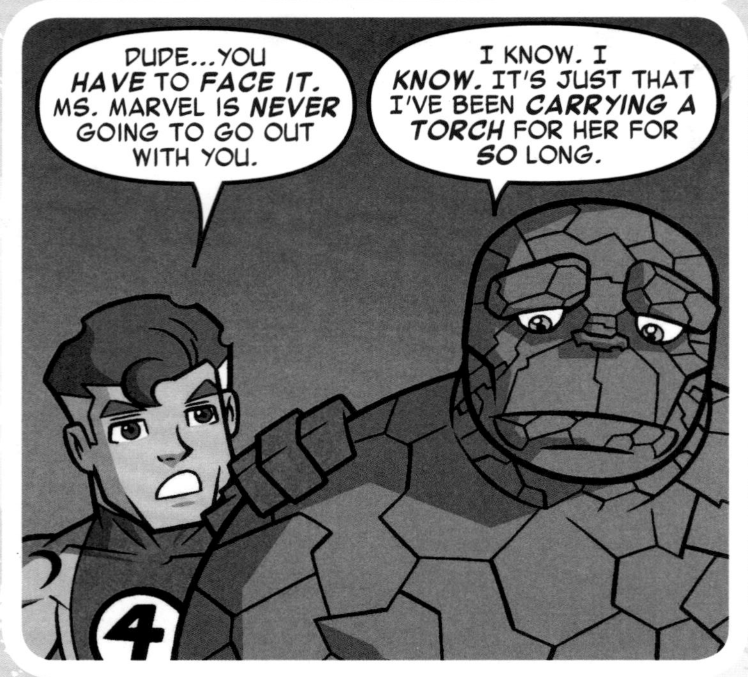
DUDE...YOU HAVE TO FACE IT. MS. MARVEL IS NEVER GOING TO GO OUT WITH YOU.
I KNOW. I KNOW. IT'S JUST THAT I'VE BEEN CARRYING A TORCH FOR HER FOR SO LONG.

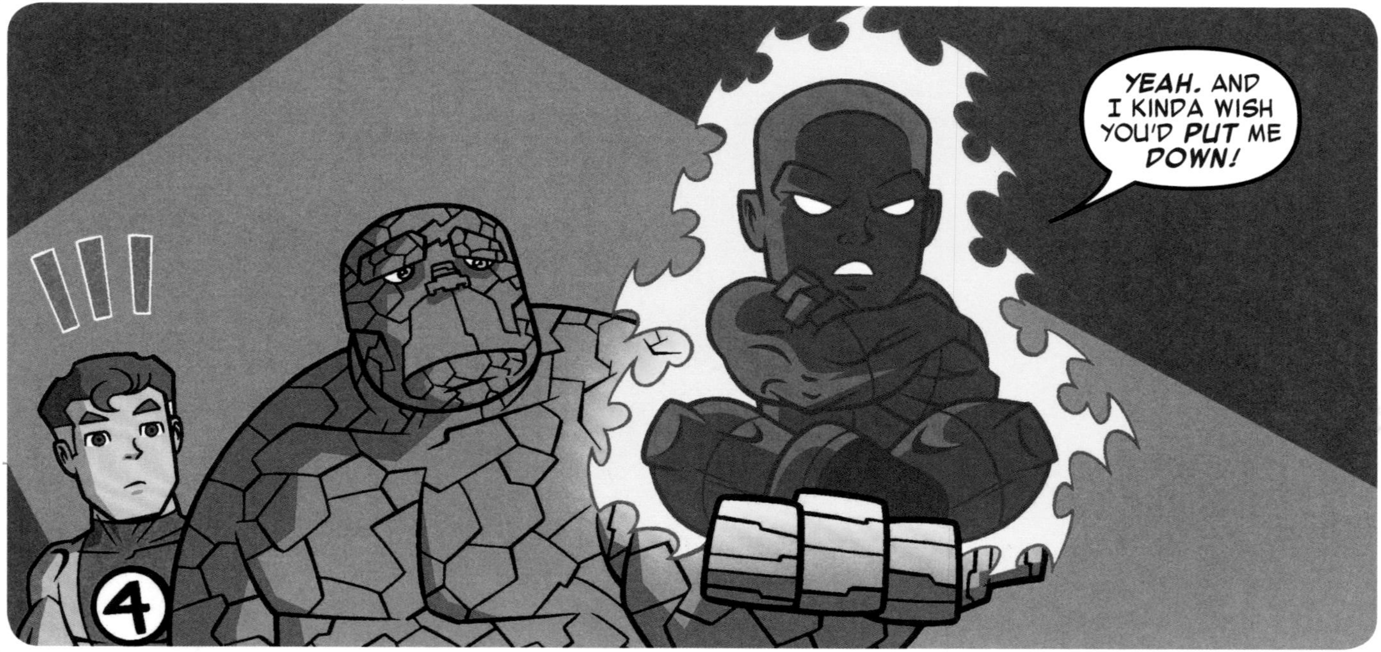
YEAH. AND I KINDA WISH YOU'D PUT ME DOWN!

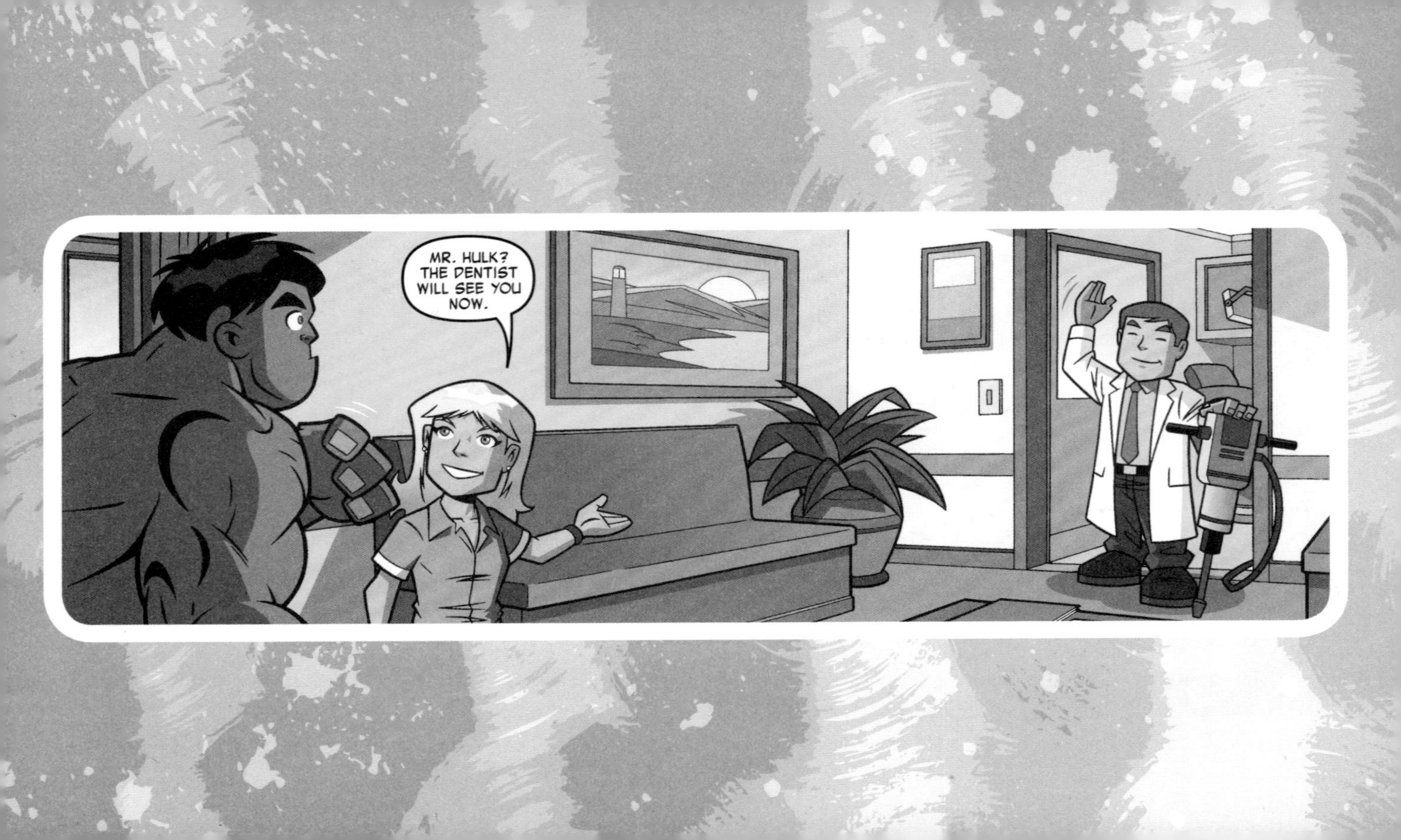
MR. HULK? THE DENTIST WILL SEE YOU NOW.

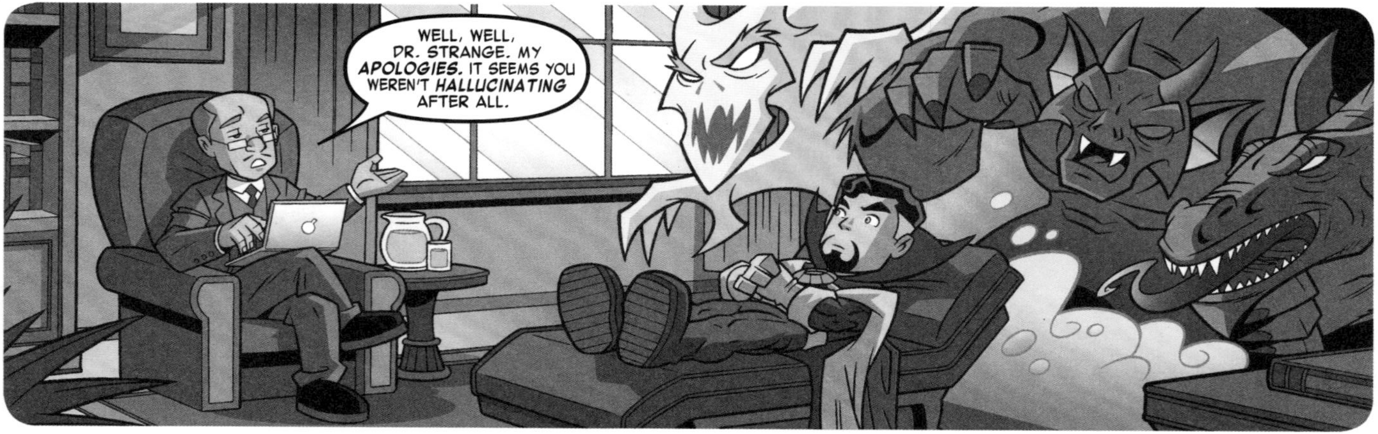
WELL, WELL, DR. STRANGE. MY *APOLOGIES.* IT SEEMS YOU WEREN'T *HALLUCINATING* AFTER ALL.

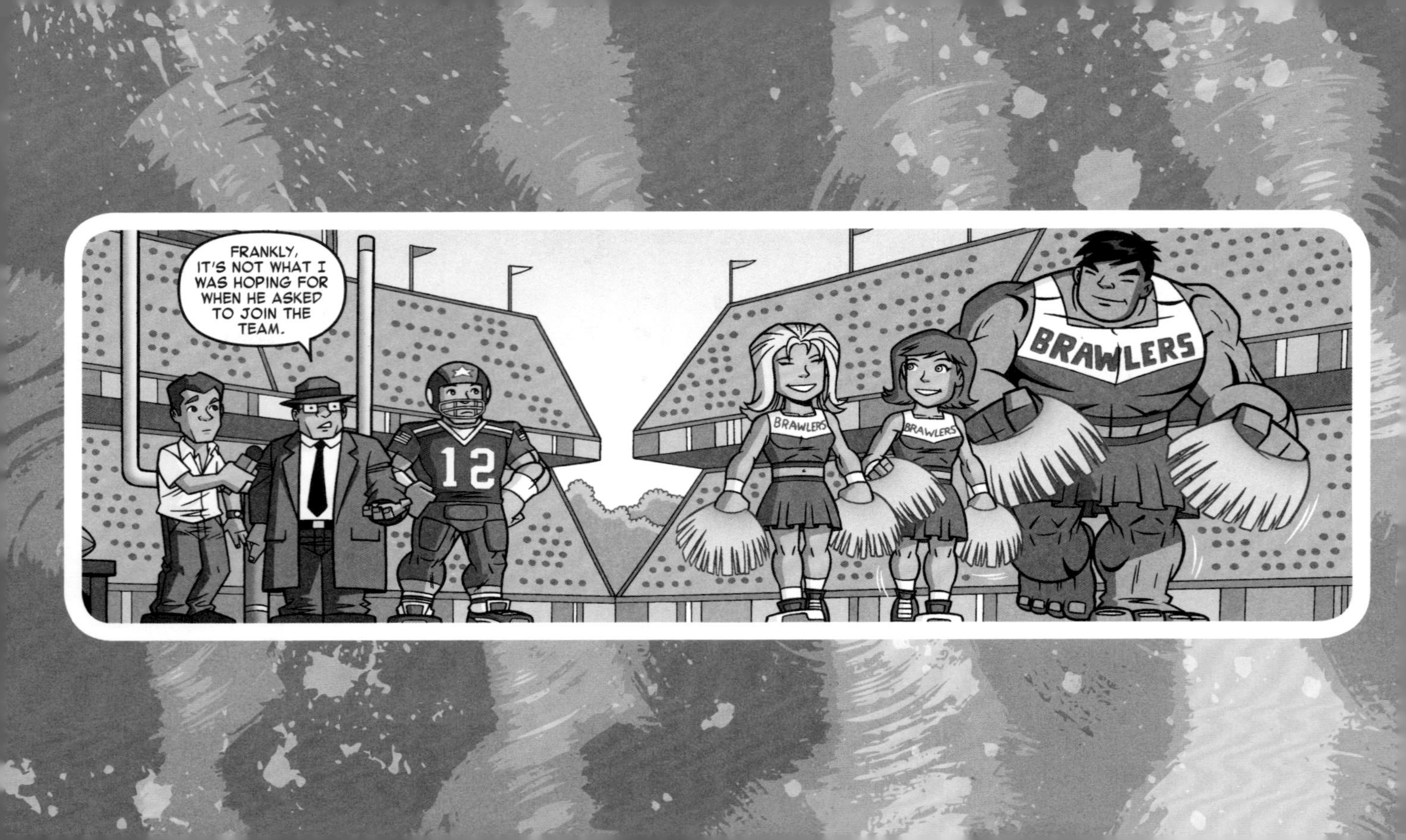
FRANKLY, IT'S NOT WHAT I WAS HOPING FOR WHEN HE ASKED TO JOIN THE TEAM.
12
BRAWLERS
BRAWLERS
BRAWLERS

SO, THAT'S ONE LARGE PIZZA WITH *EVERYTHING* ON IT.
COSMIC PIZZA

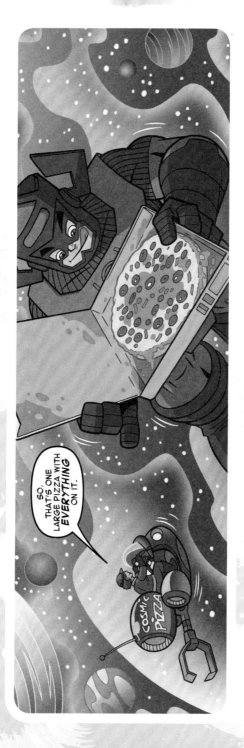

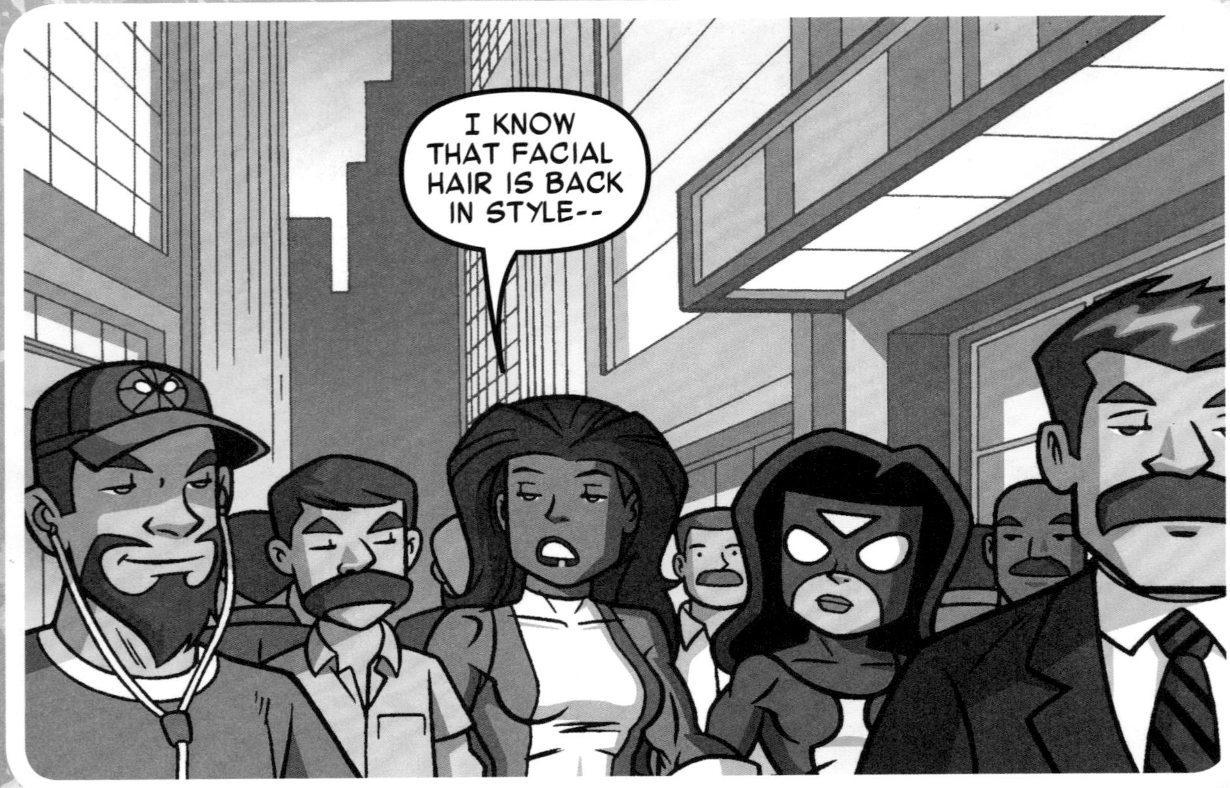
I KNOW THAT FACIAL HAIR IS BACK IN STYLE--

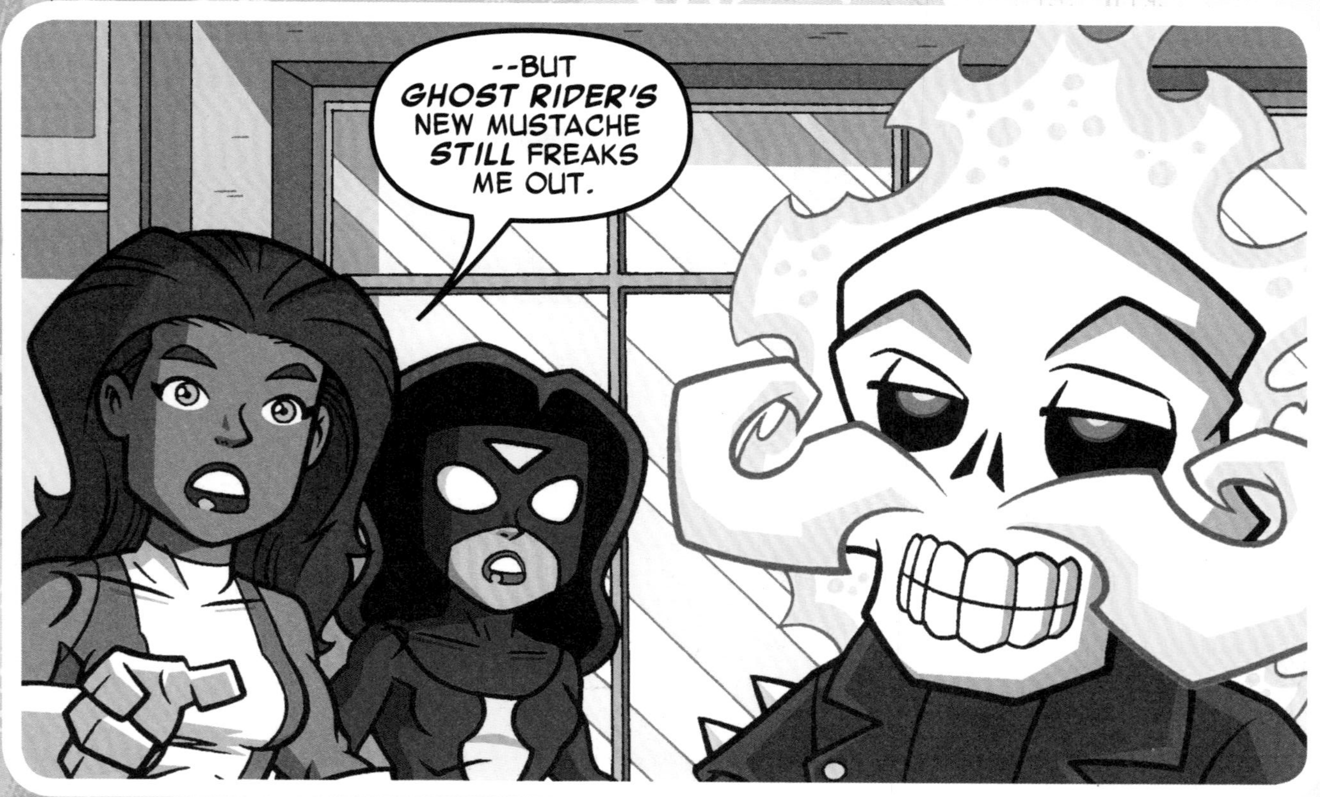
--BUT GHOST RIDER'S NEW MUSTACHE STILL FREAKS ME OUT.

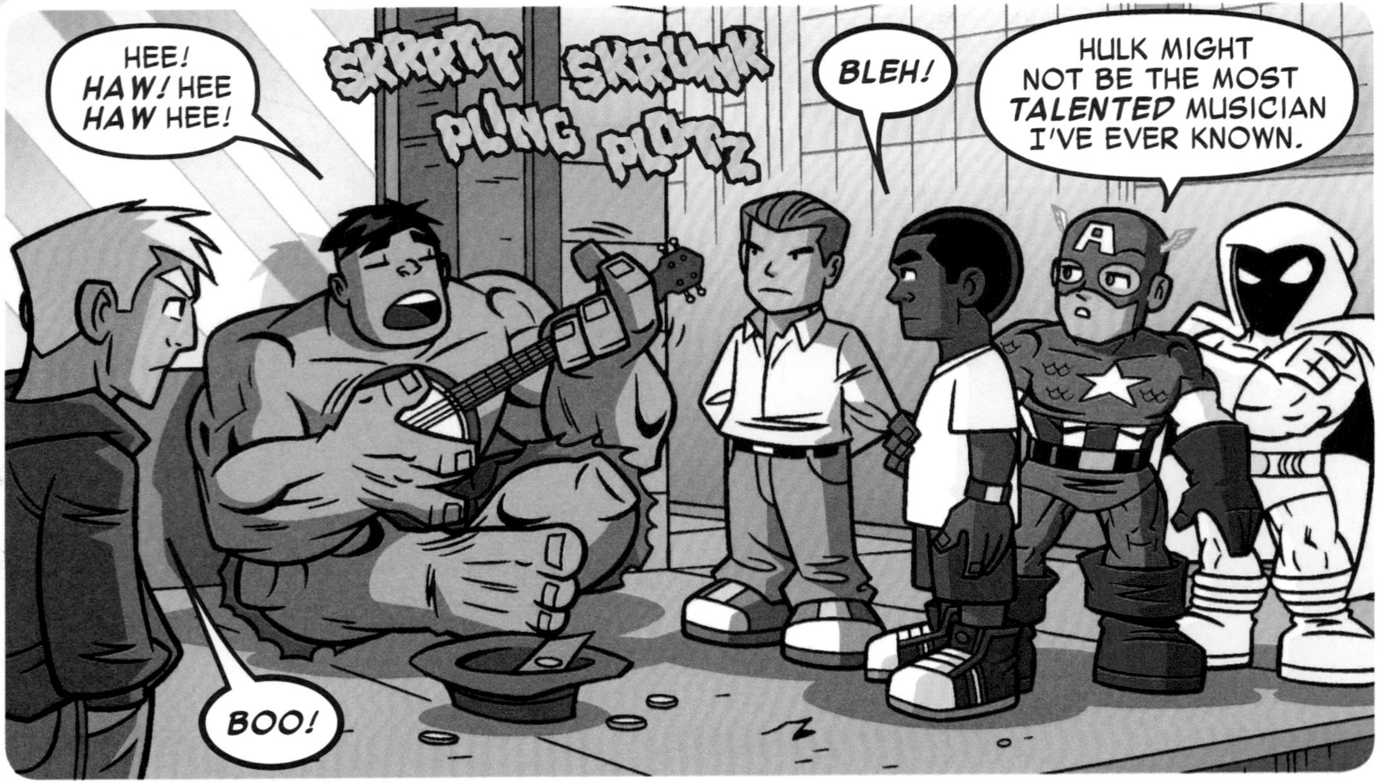
HEE! HAW! HEE HAW HEE!
SKRRTT SKRUNK PL!NG PLOTTZ
BLEH!
HULK MIGHT NOT BE THE MOST TALENTED MUSICIAN I'VE EVER KNOWN.
BOO!

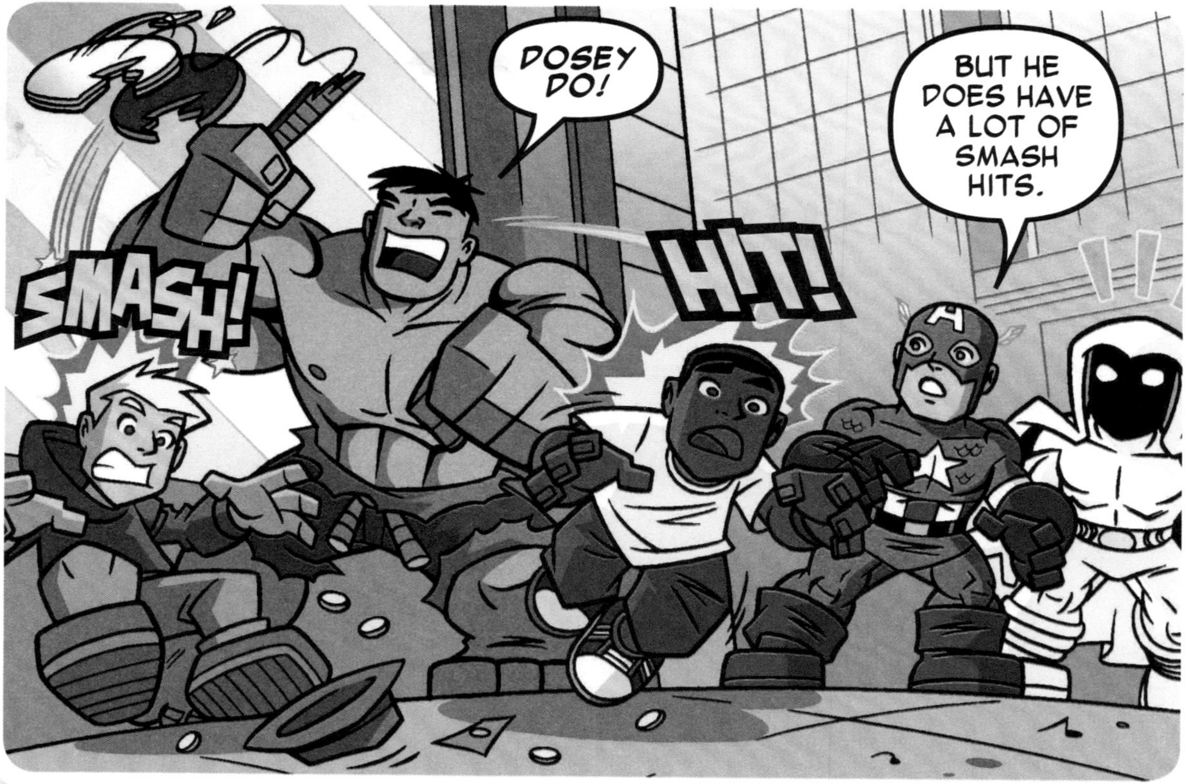
SMASH!
DOSEY DO!
HIT!
BUT HE DOES HAVE A LOT OF SMASH HITS.

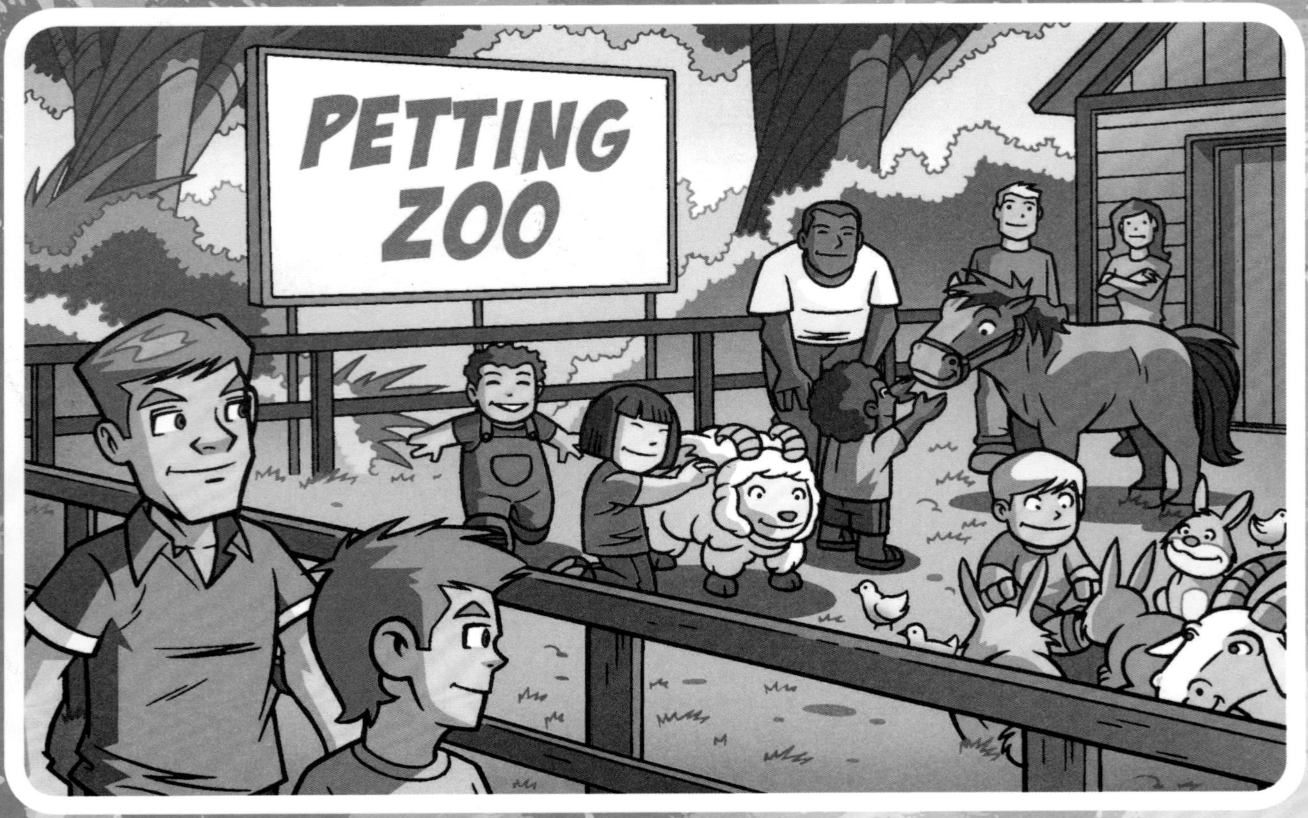
PETTING ZOO

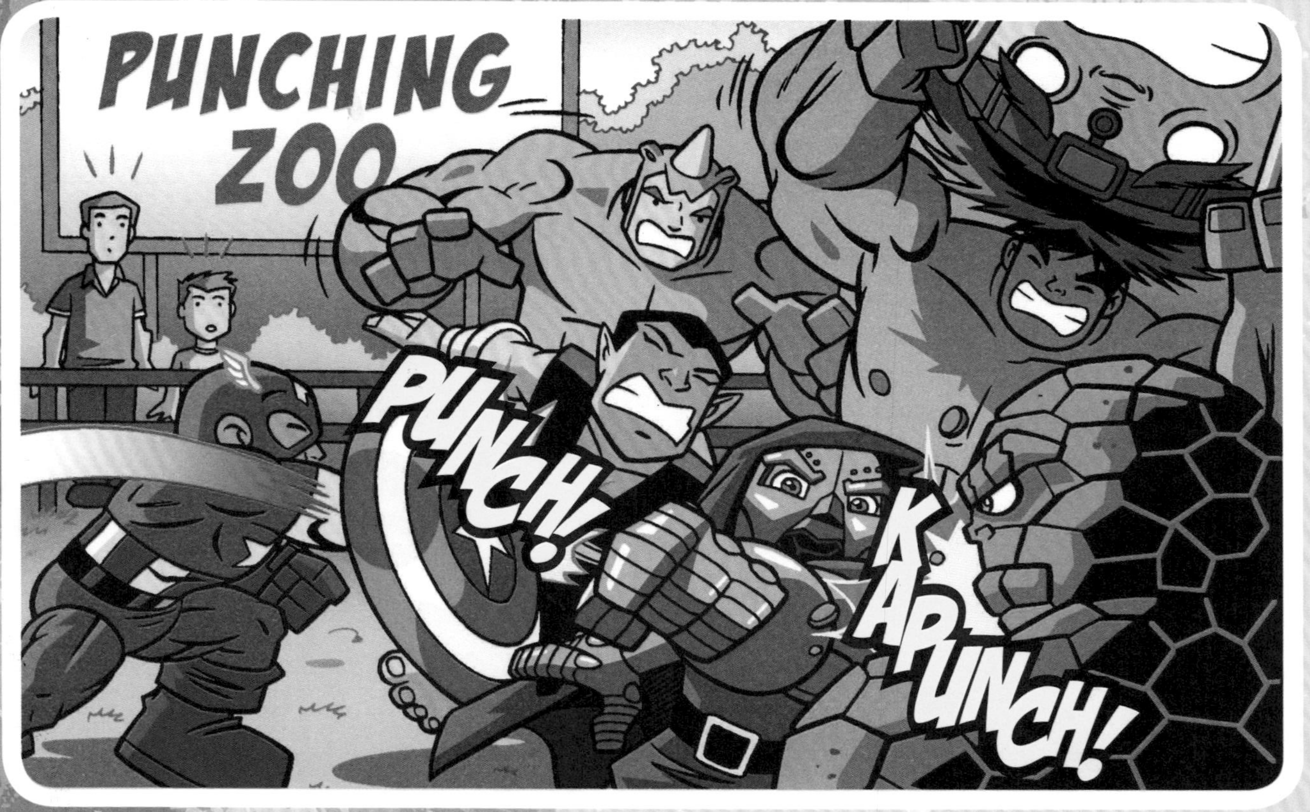
PUNCHING ZOO
PUNCH!
KAPUNCH!

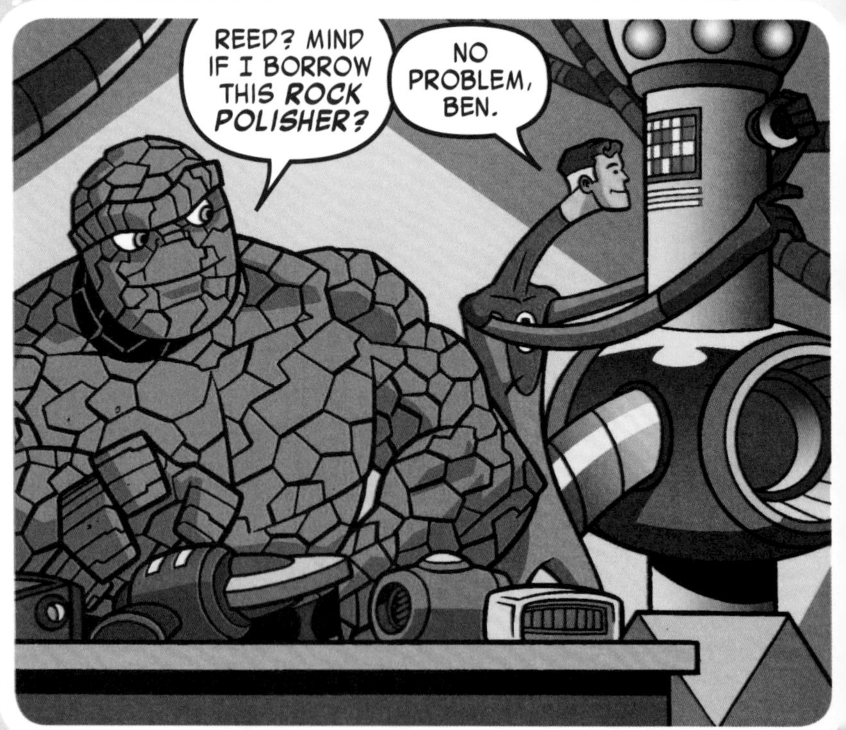
REED? MIND IF I BORROW THIS ROCK POLISHER?
NO PROBLEM, BEN.

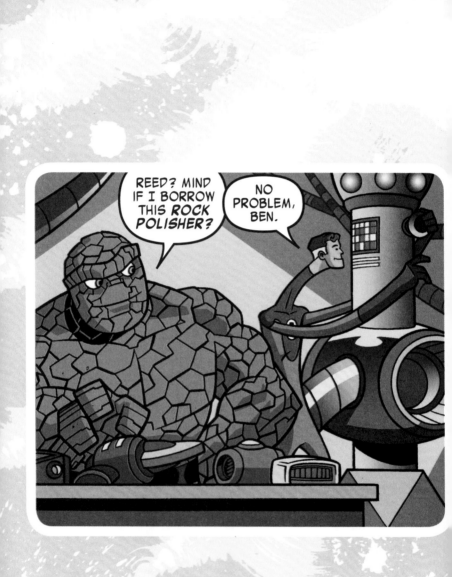

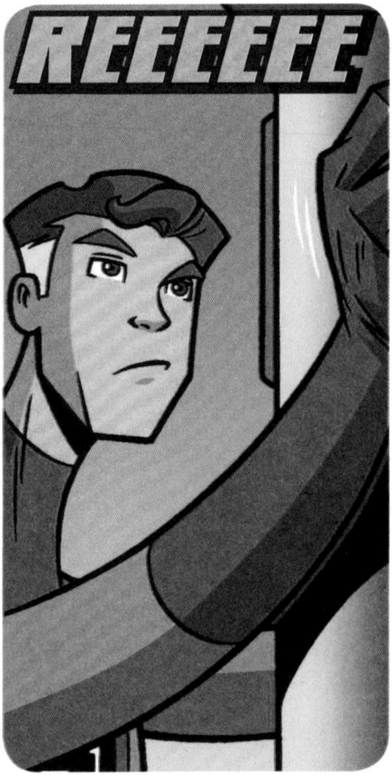
REEEEEE

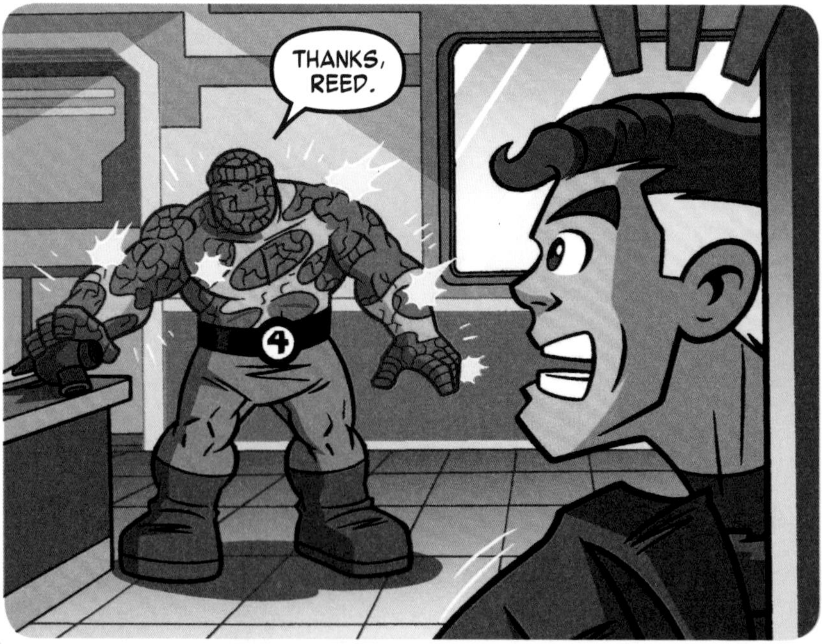
THANKS, REED.

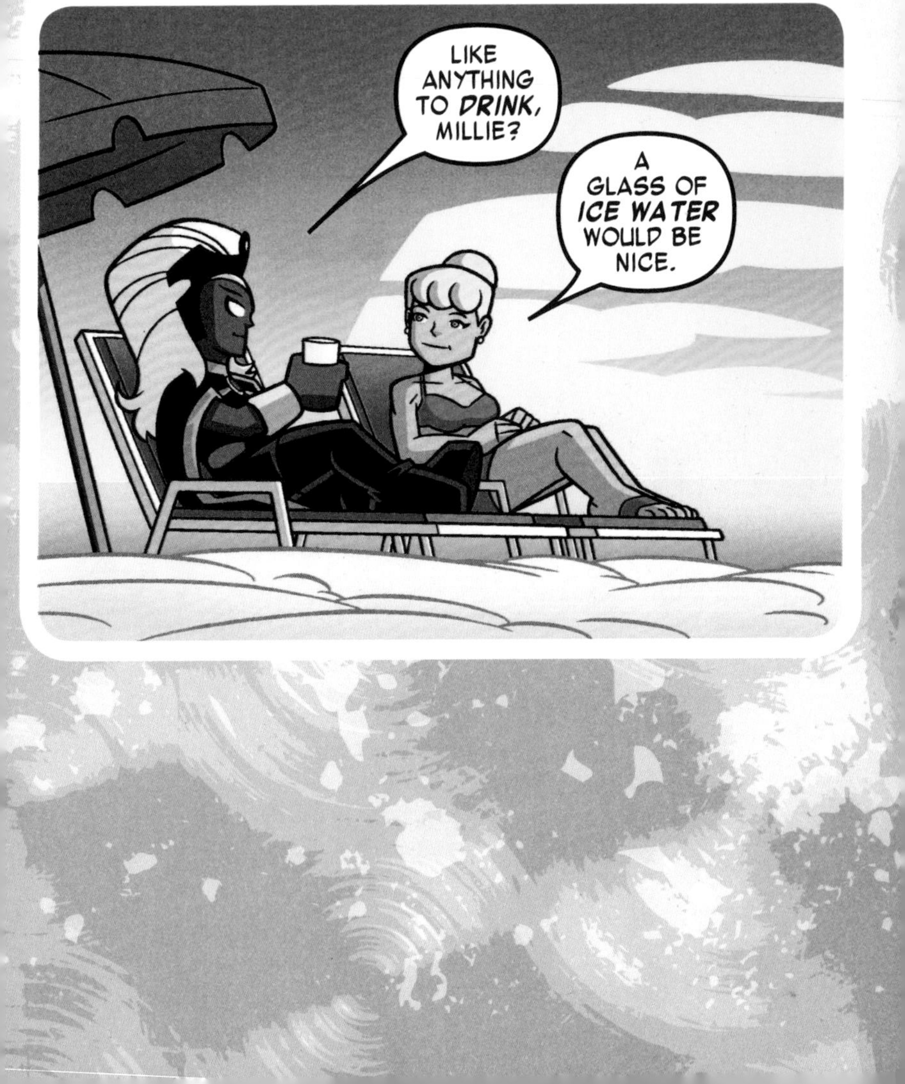
LIKE ANYTHING TO DRINK, MILLIE?
A GLASS OF ICE WATER WOULD BE NICE.

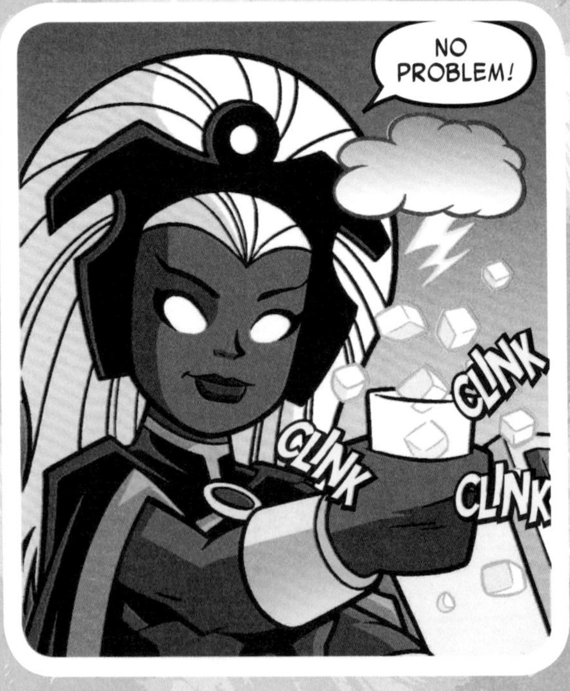
NO PROBLEM!
CLINK
CLINK
CLINK

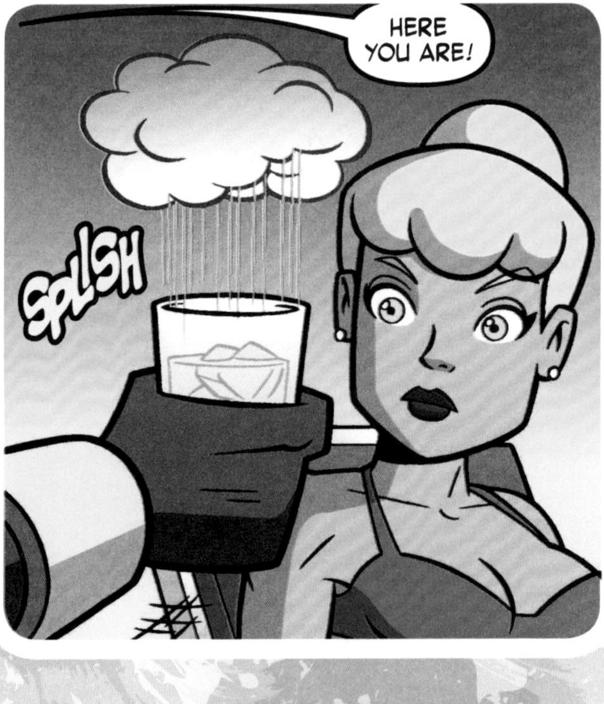
HERE YOU ARE!
SPLISH

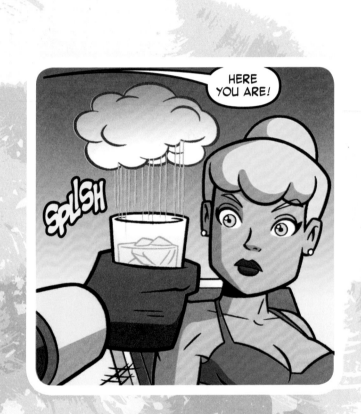

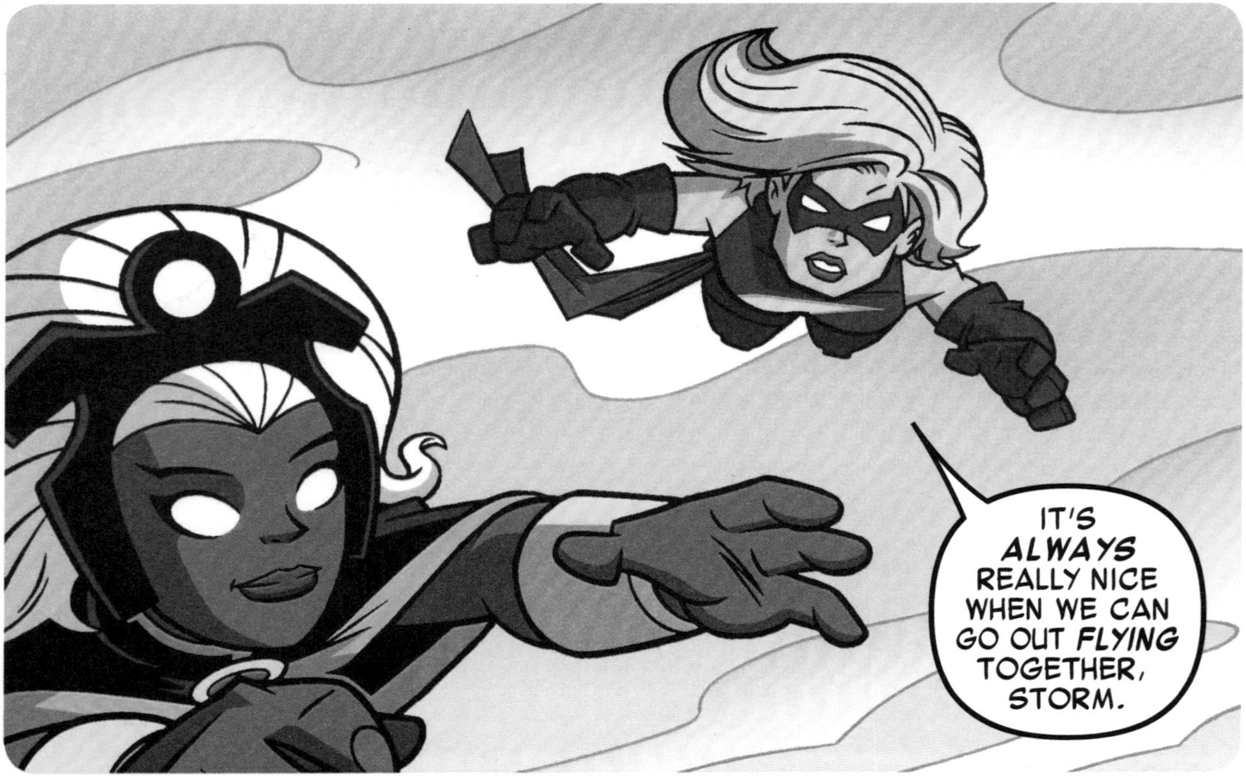
IT'S *ALWAYS* REALLY NICE WHEN WE CAN GO OUT *FLYING* TOGETHER, STORM.

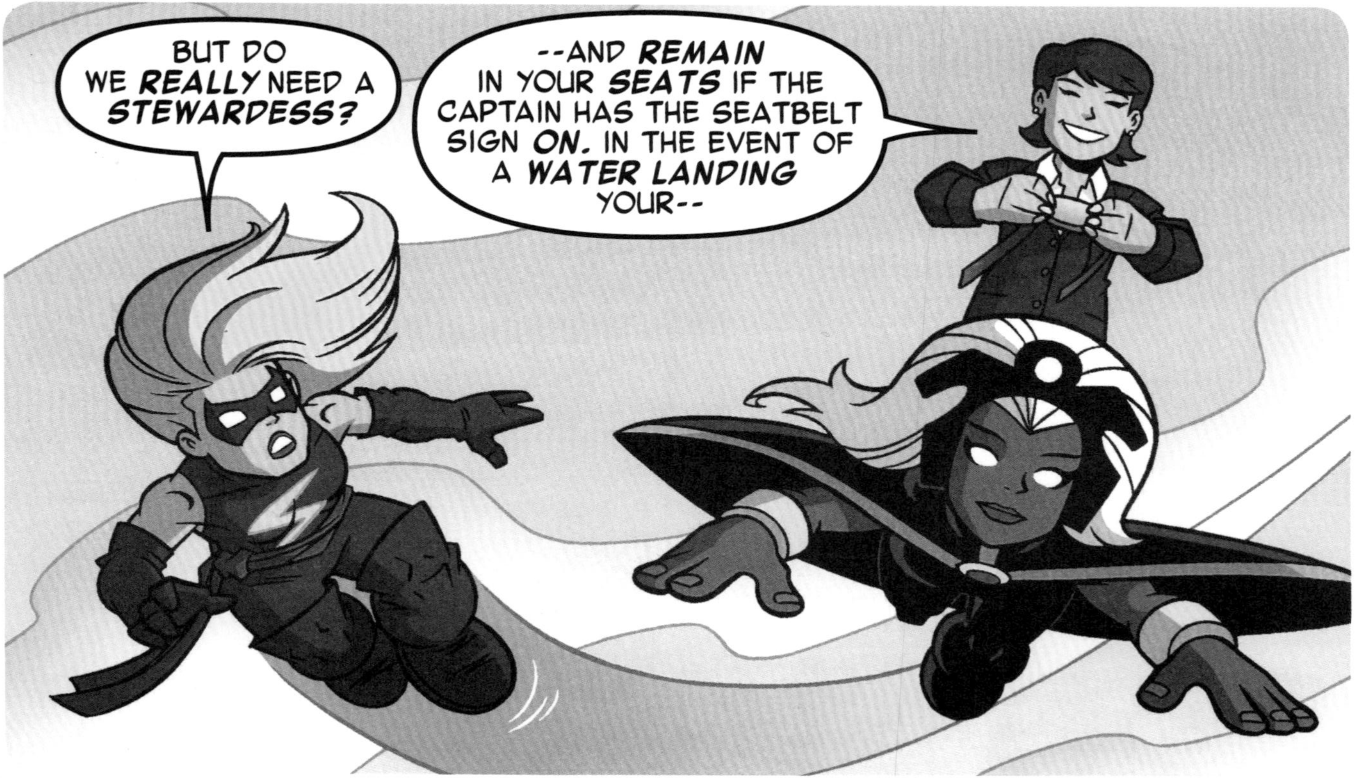
BUT DO WE REALLY NEED A STEWARDESS?
--AND REMAIN IN YOUR SEATS IF THE CAPTAIN HAS THE SEATBELT SIGN ON. IN THE EVENT OF A WATER LANDING YOUR--

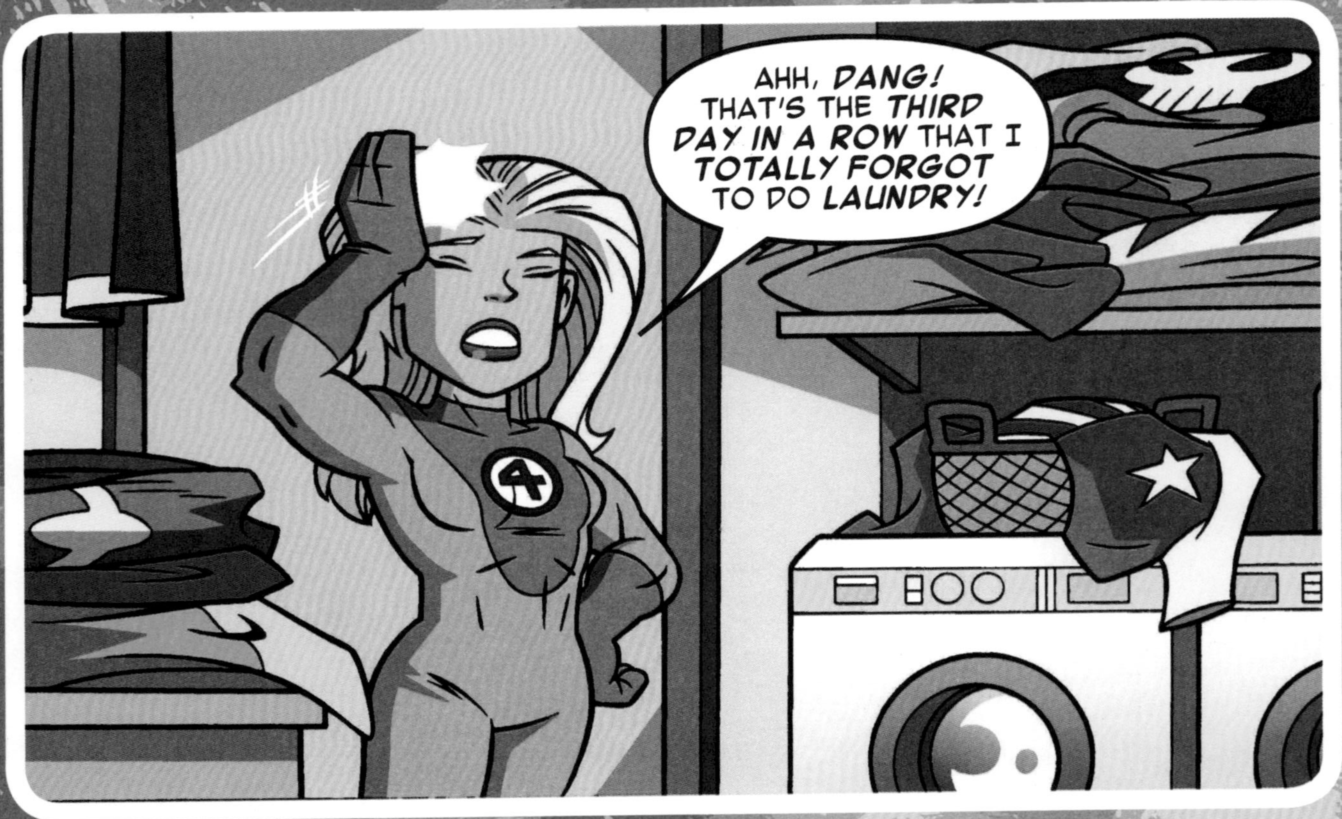
AHH, DANG! THAT'S THE THIRD DAY IN A ROW THAT I TOTALLY FORGOT TO DO LAUNDRY!

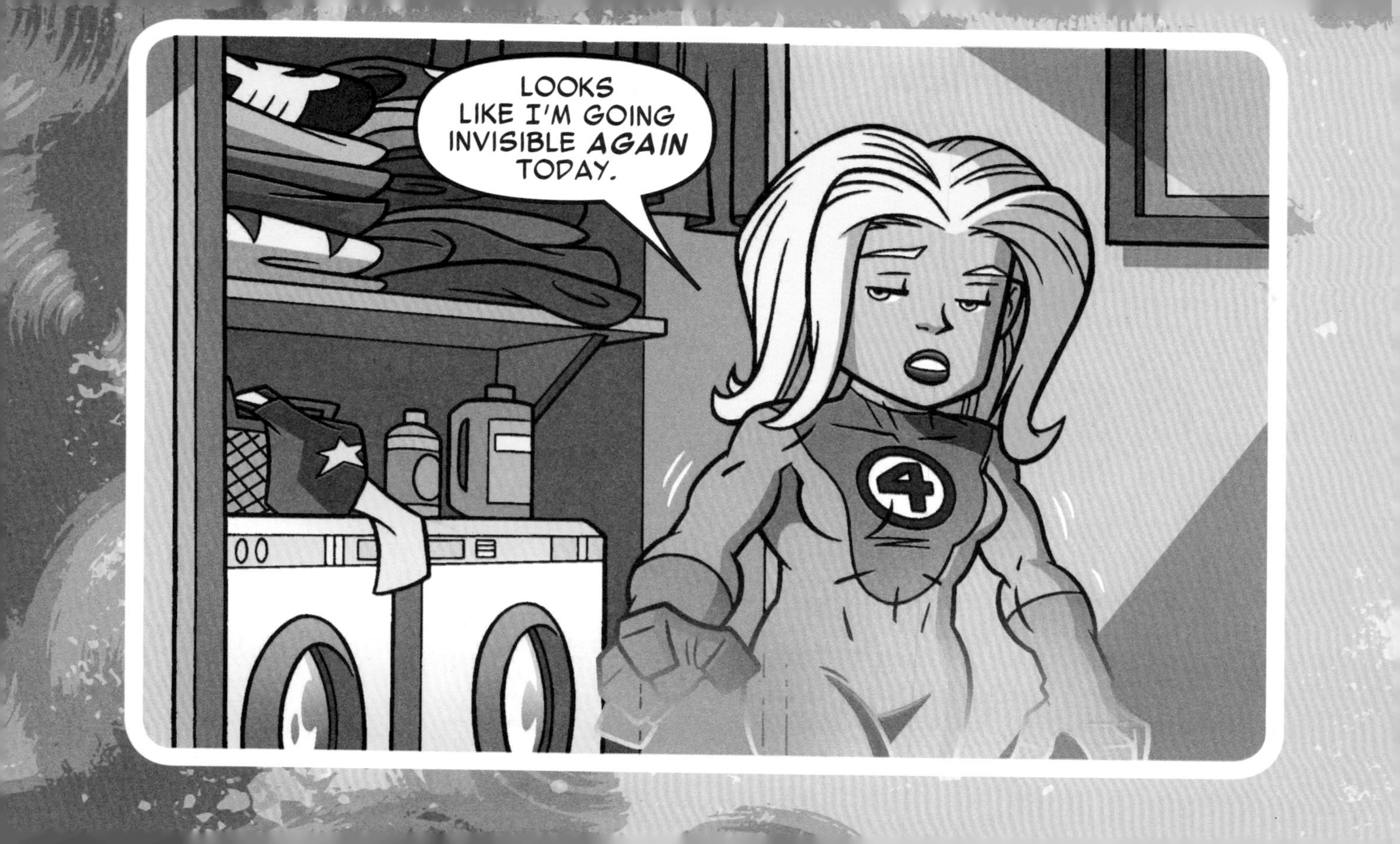
LOOKS LIKE I'M GOING INVISIBLE AGAIN TODAY.

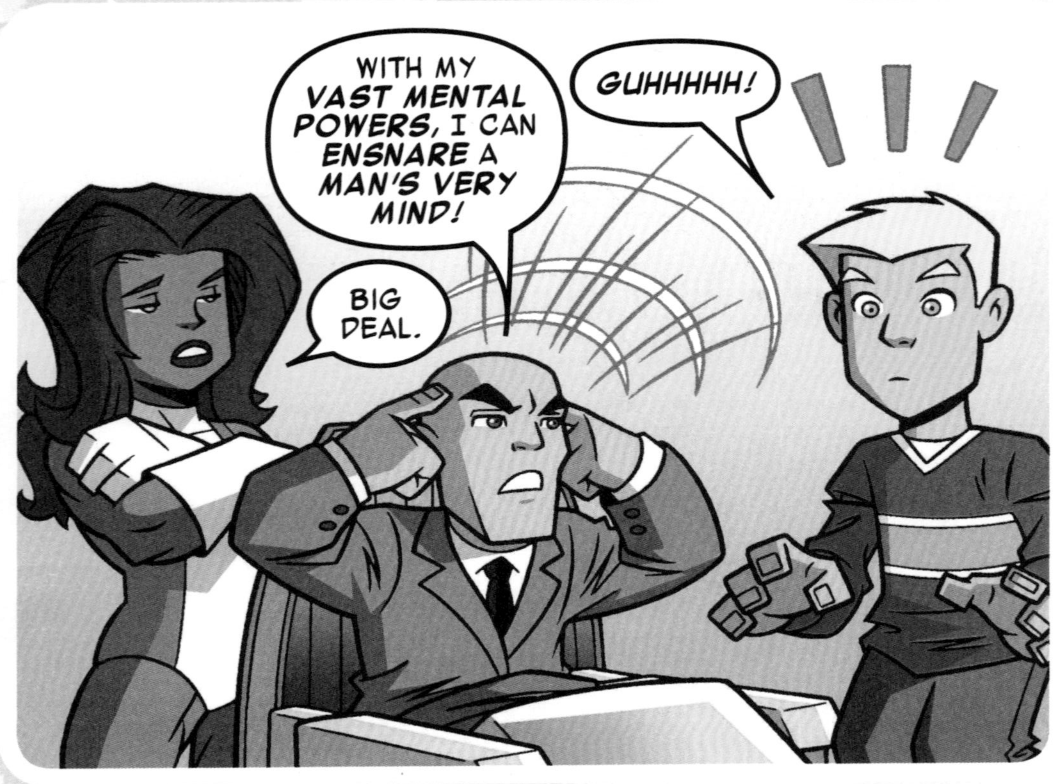
WITH MY VAST MENTAL POWERS, I CAN ENSNARE A MAN'S VERY MIND!
BIG DEAL.
GUHHHHH!

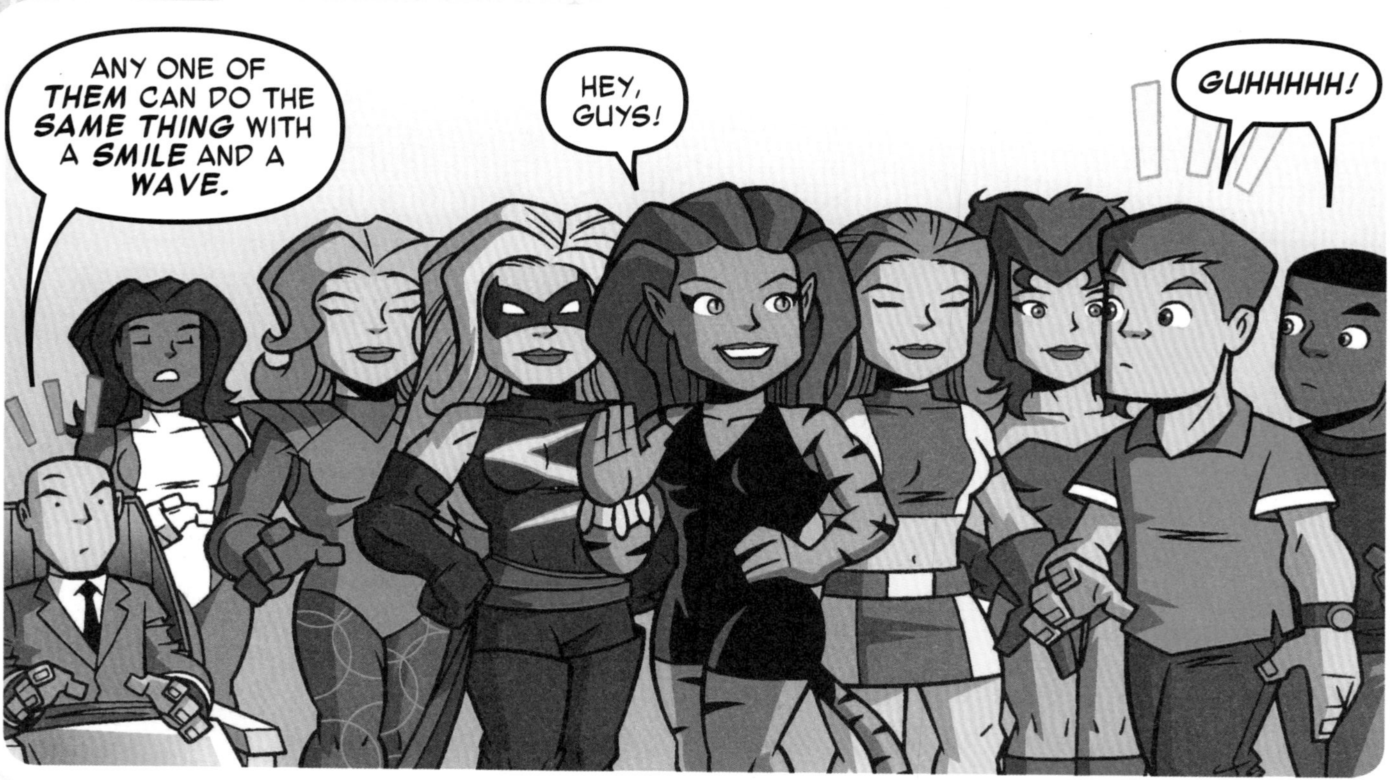
ANY ONE OF THEM CAN DO THE SAME THING WITH A SMILE AND A WAVE.
HEY, GUYS!
GUHHHHH!

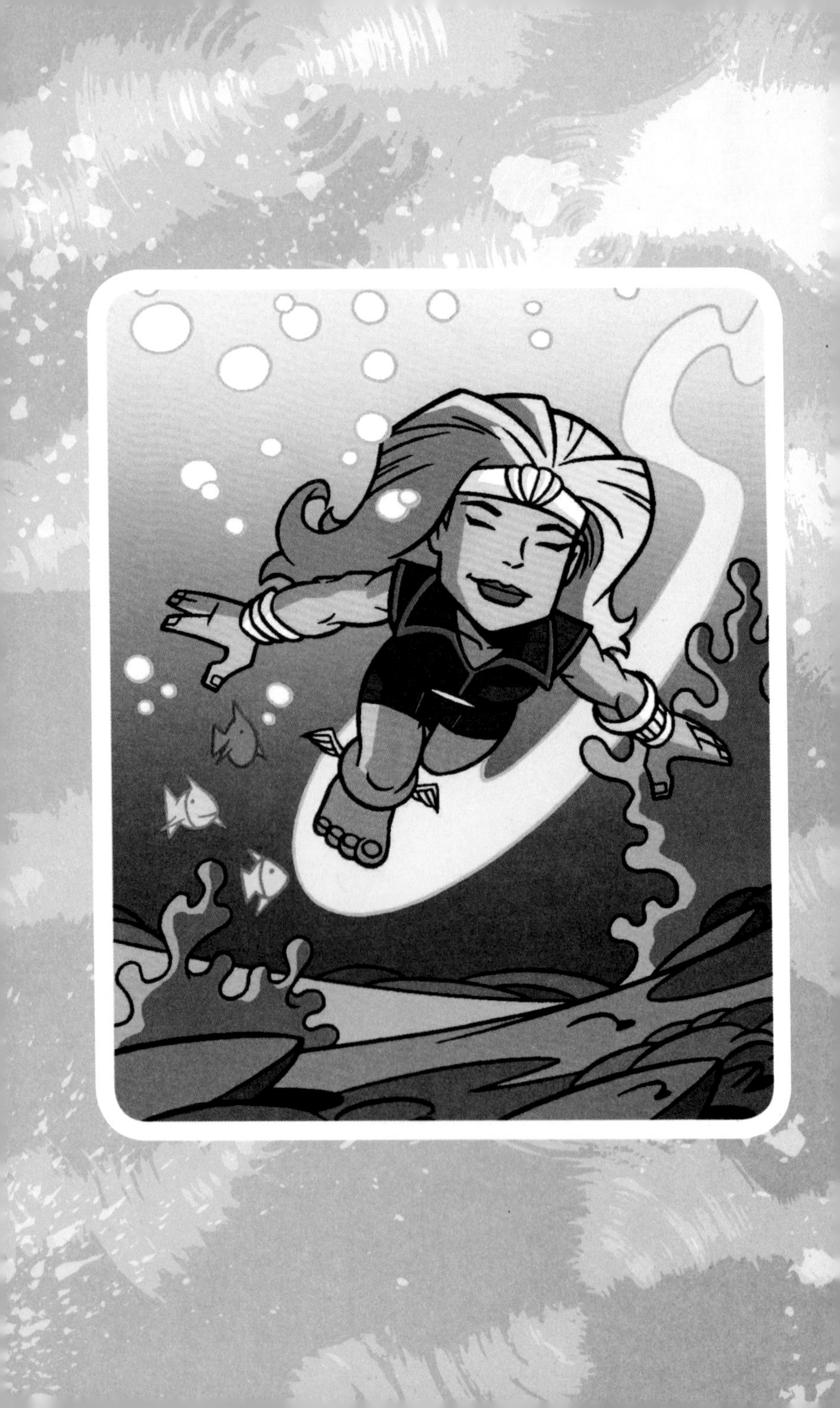

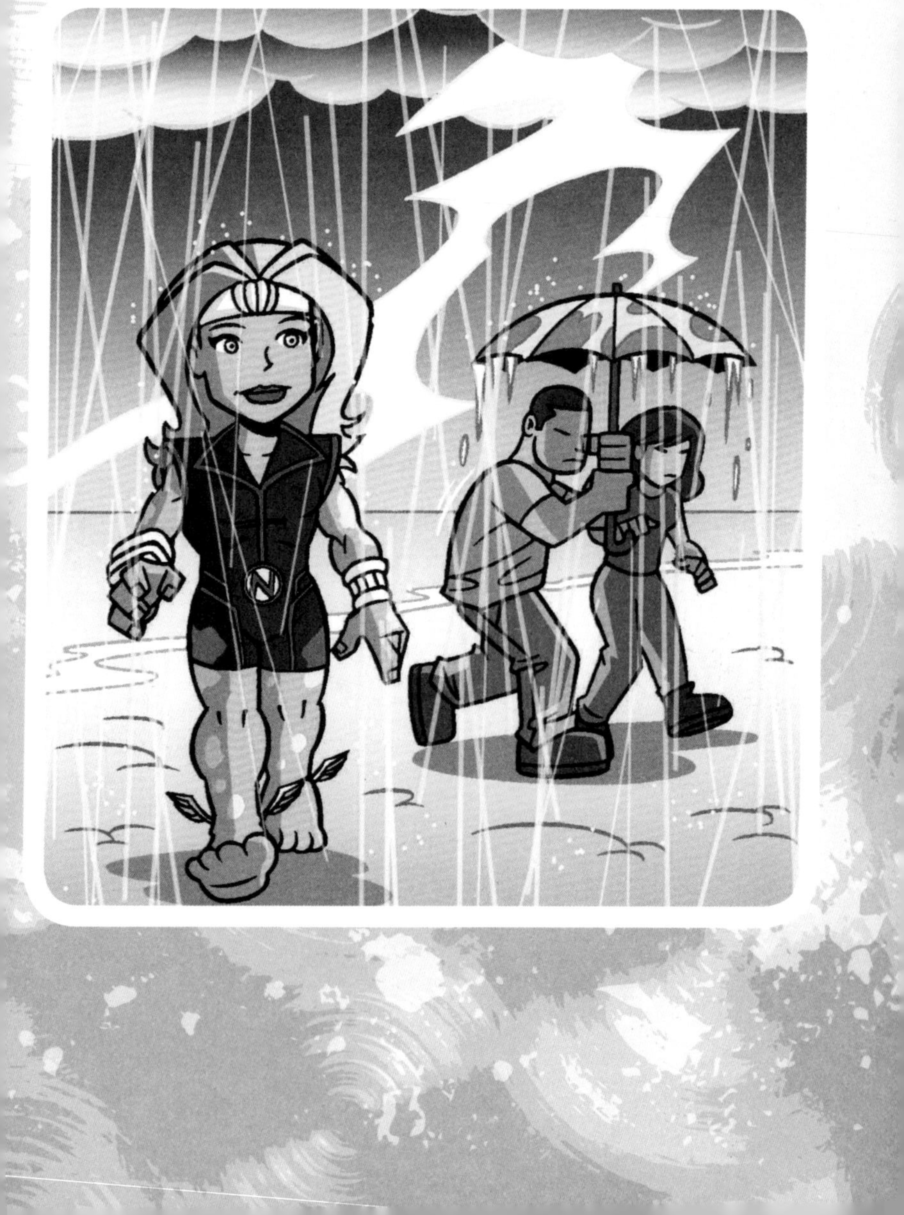

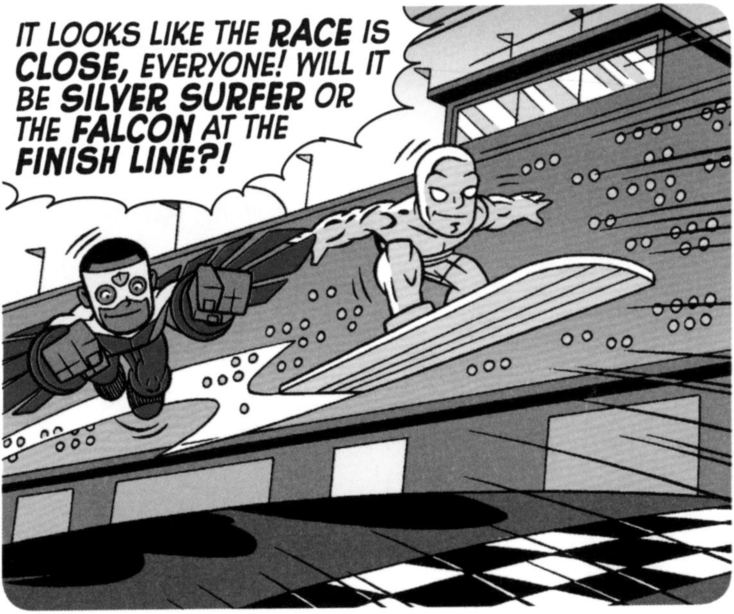
IT LOOKS LIKE THE RACE IS CLOSE, EVERYONE! WILL IT BE SILVER SURFER OR THE FALCON AT THE FINISH LINE?!

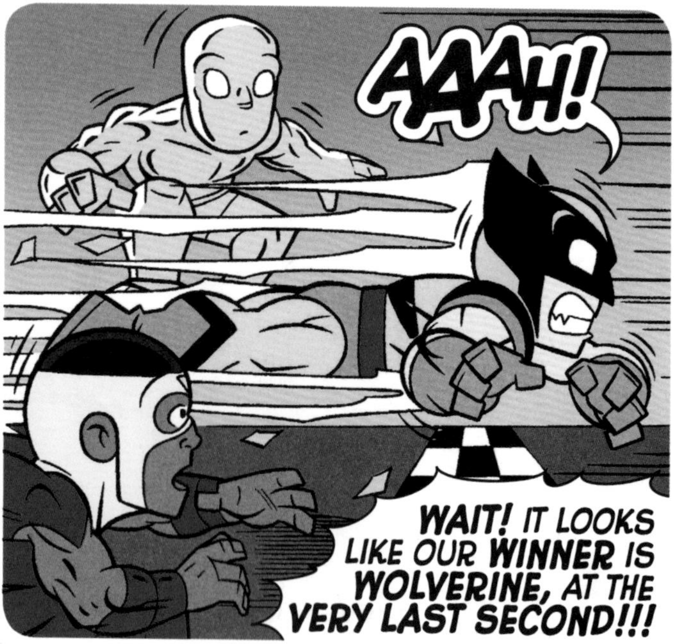
AAAH!
WAIT! IT LOOKS LIKE OUR WINNER IS WOLVERINE, AT THE VERY LAST SECOND!!!

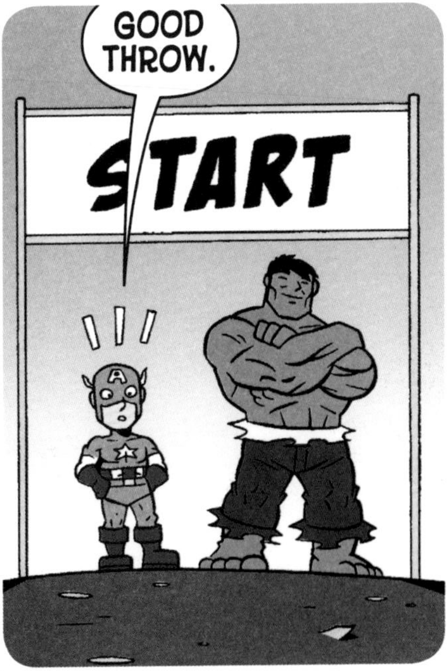
GOOD THROW.
START

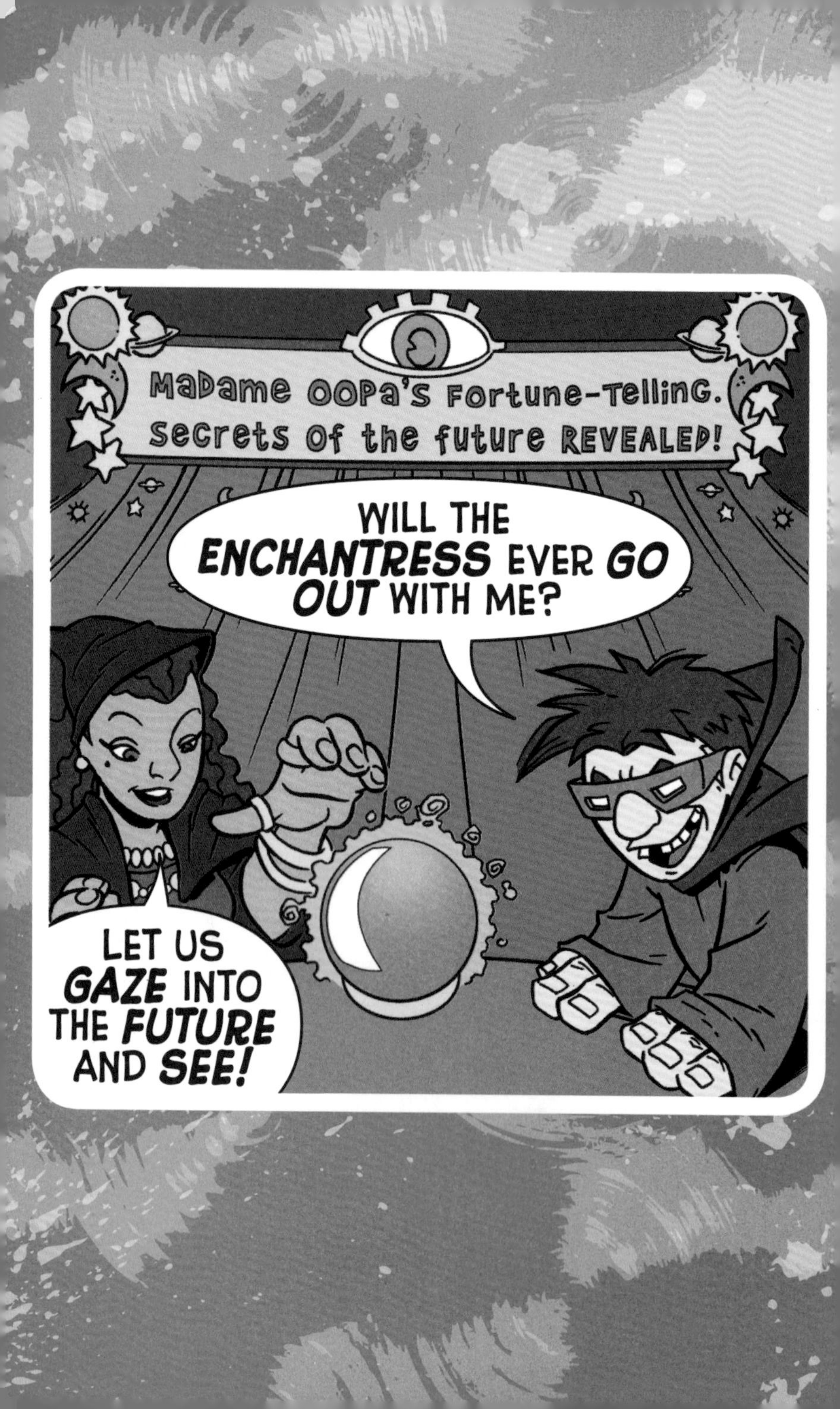
MADAME OOPA'S FORTUNE-TELLING.
SECRETS OF THE FUTURE REVEALED!
WILL THE ENCHANTRESS EVER GO OUT WITH ME?
LET US GAZE INTO THE FUTURE AND SEE!

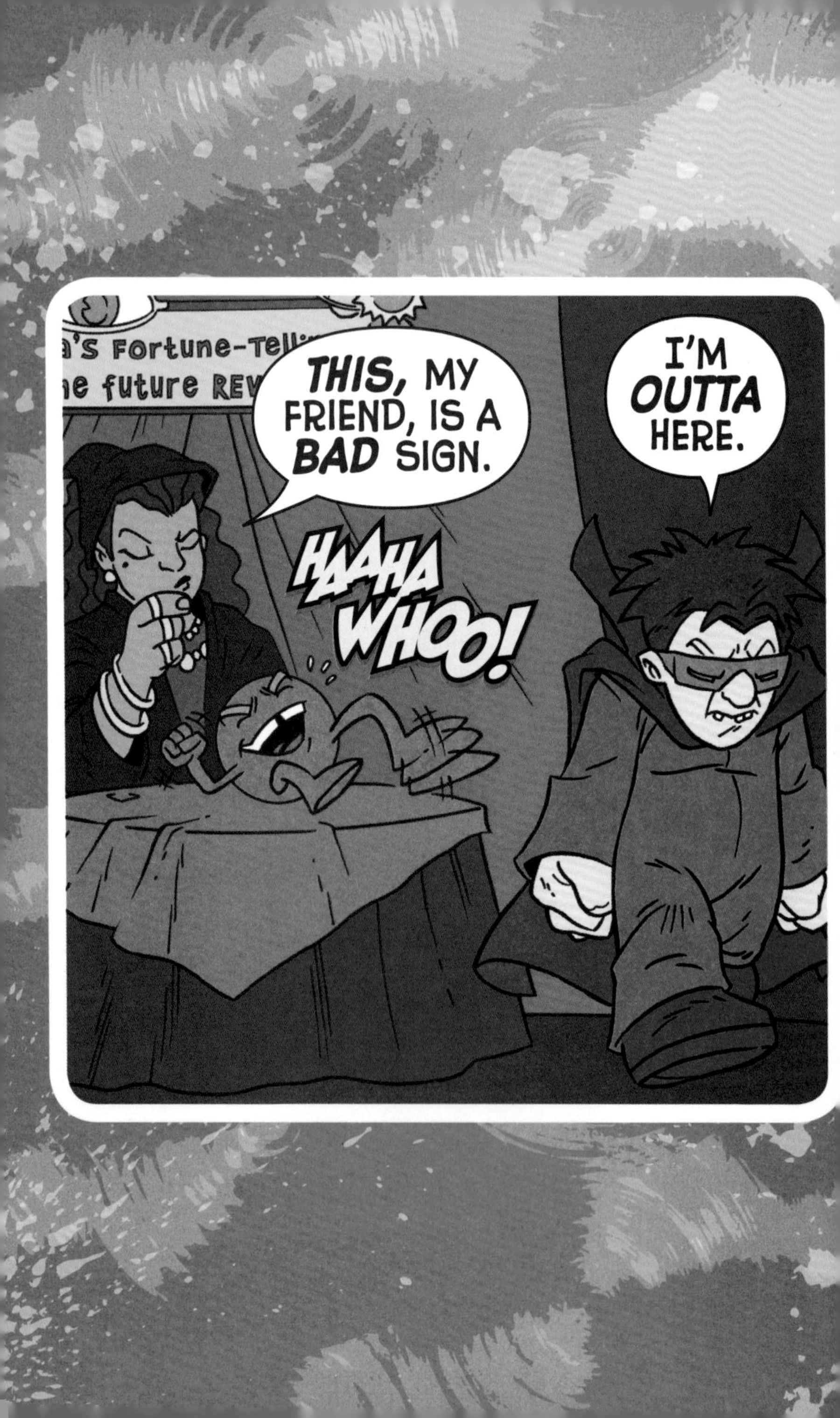
a'S Fortune-Tell
e future REV
THIS, MY FRIEND, IS A BAD SIGN.
HAAHA WHOO!
I'M OUTTA HERE.

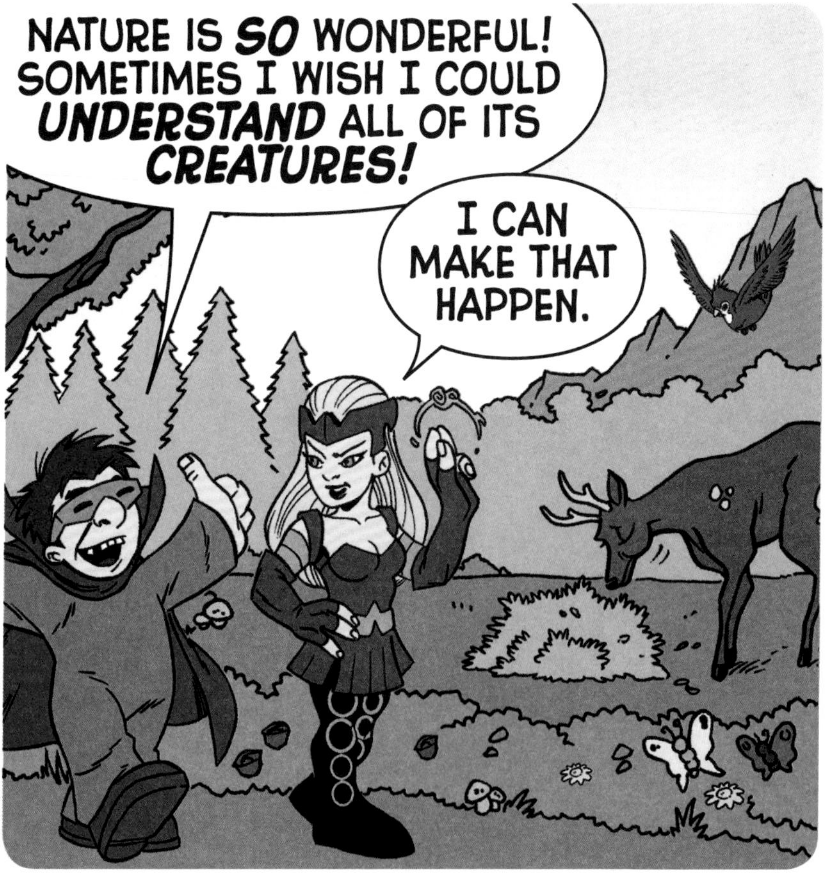
NATURE IS SO WONDERFUL! SOMETIMES I WISH I COULD UNDERSTAND ALL OF ITS CREATURES!
I CAN MAKE THAT HAPPEN.

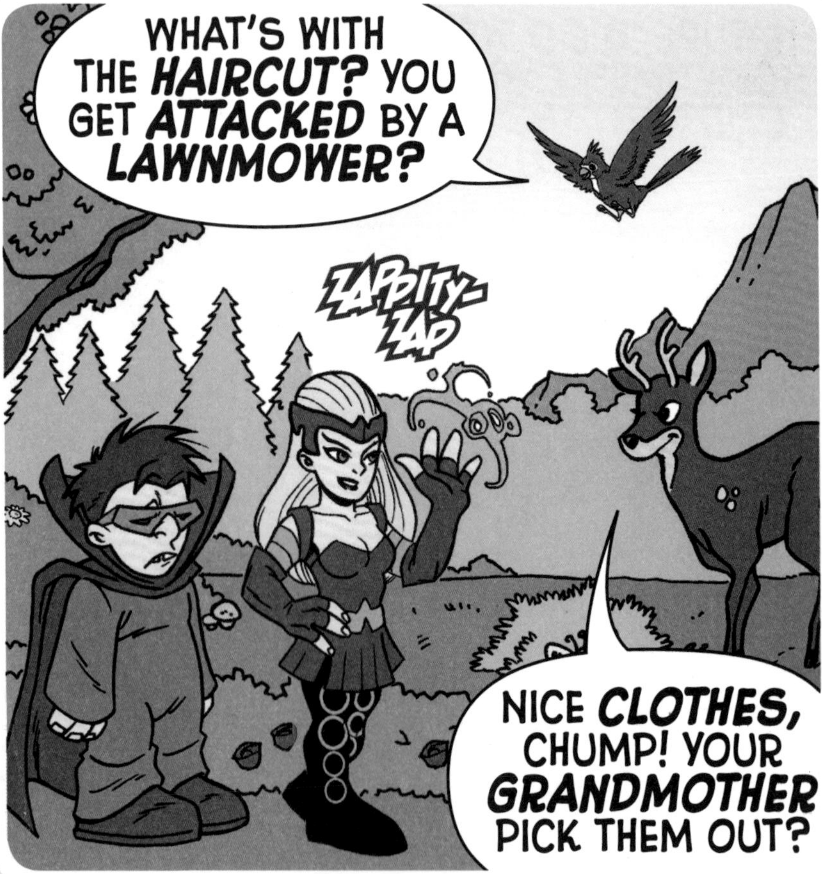
WHAT'S WITH THE HAIRCUT? YOU GET ATTACKED BY A LAWNMOWER?
ZAPPITY-ZAP
NICE CLOTHES, CHUMP! YOUR GRANDMOTHER PICK THEM OUT?

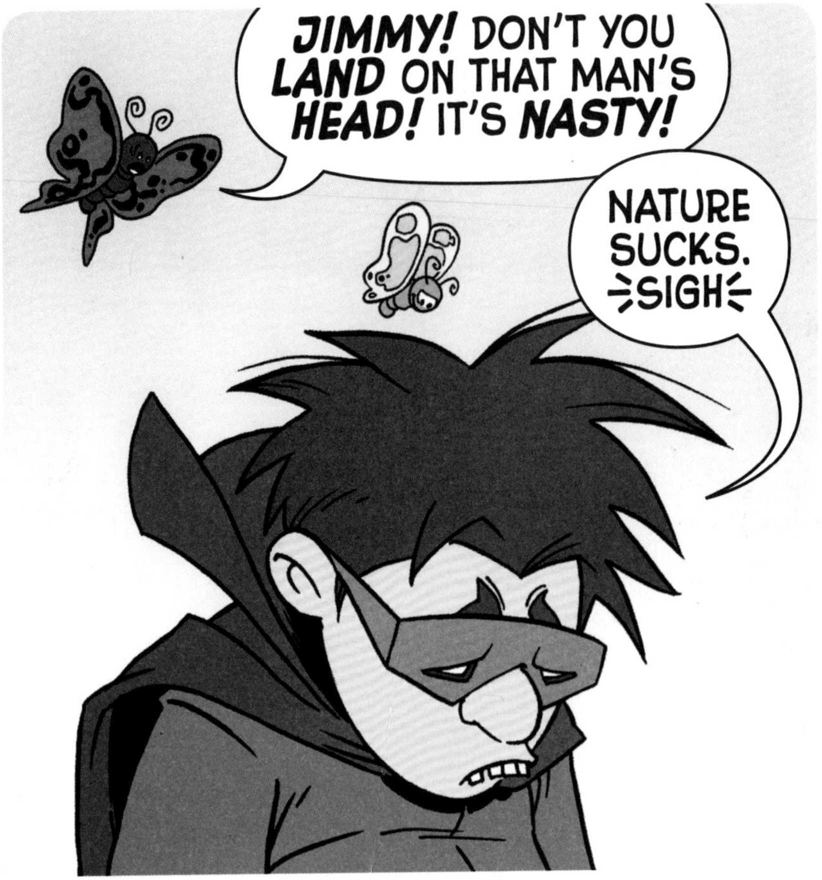
JIMMY! DON'T YOU LAND ON THAT MAN'S HEAD! IT'S NASTY!
NATURE SUCKS. SIGH

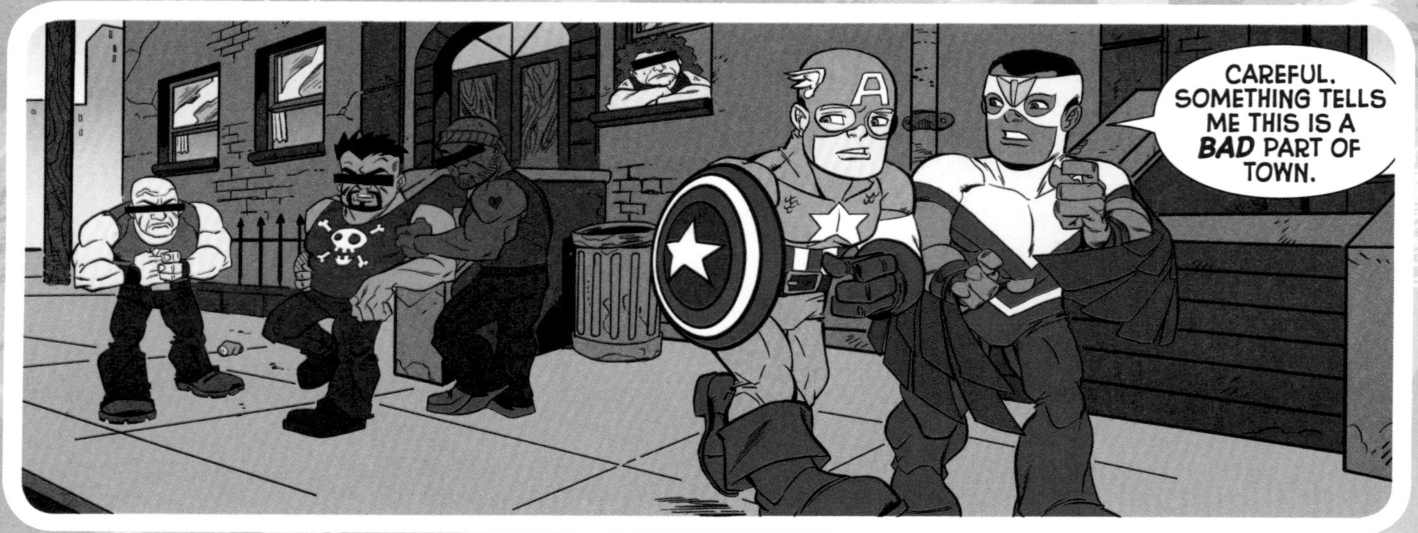
CAREFUL. SOMETHING TELLS ME THIS IS A ***BAD*** PART OF TOWN.

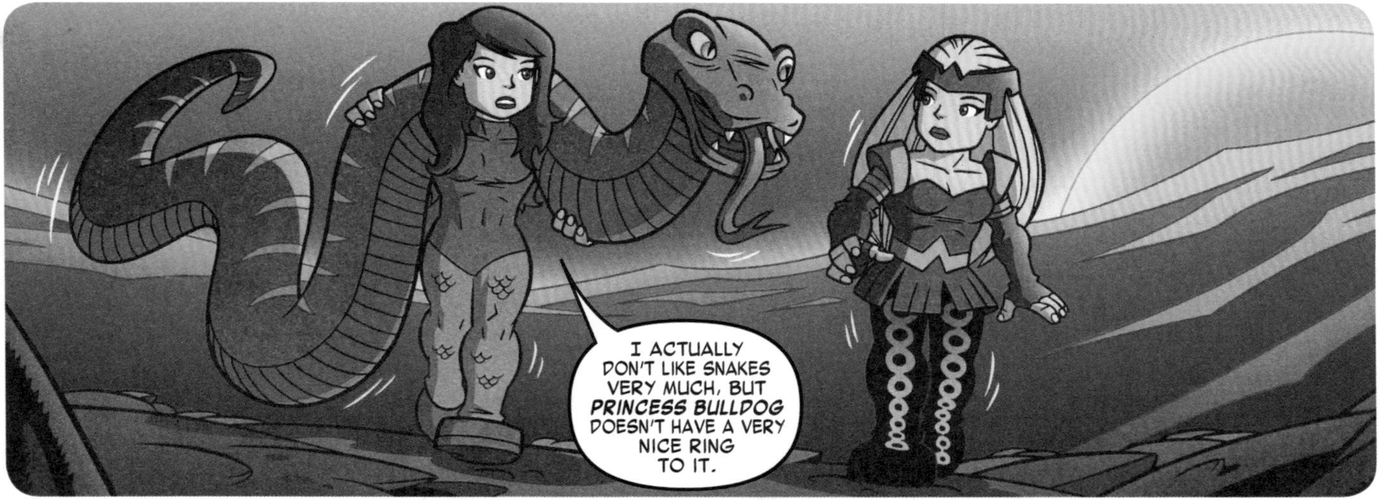
I ACTUALLY DON'T LIKE SNAKES VERY MUCH, BUT ***PRINCESS BULLDOG*** DOESN'T HAVE A VERY NICE RING TO IT.

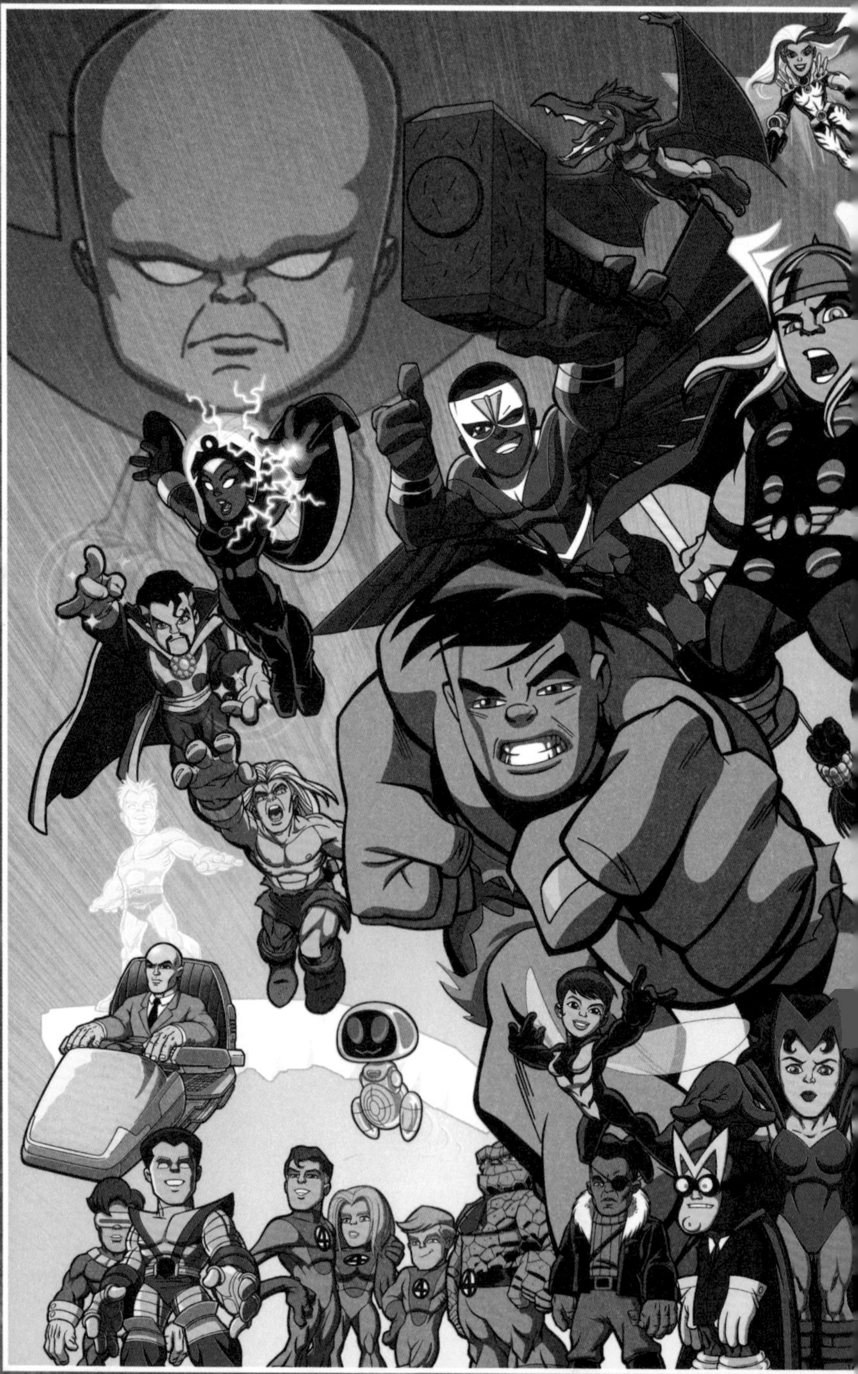

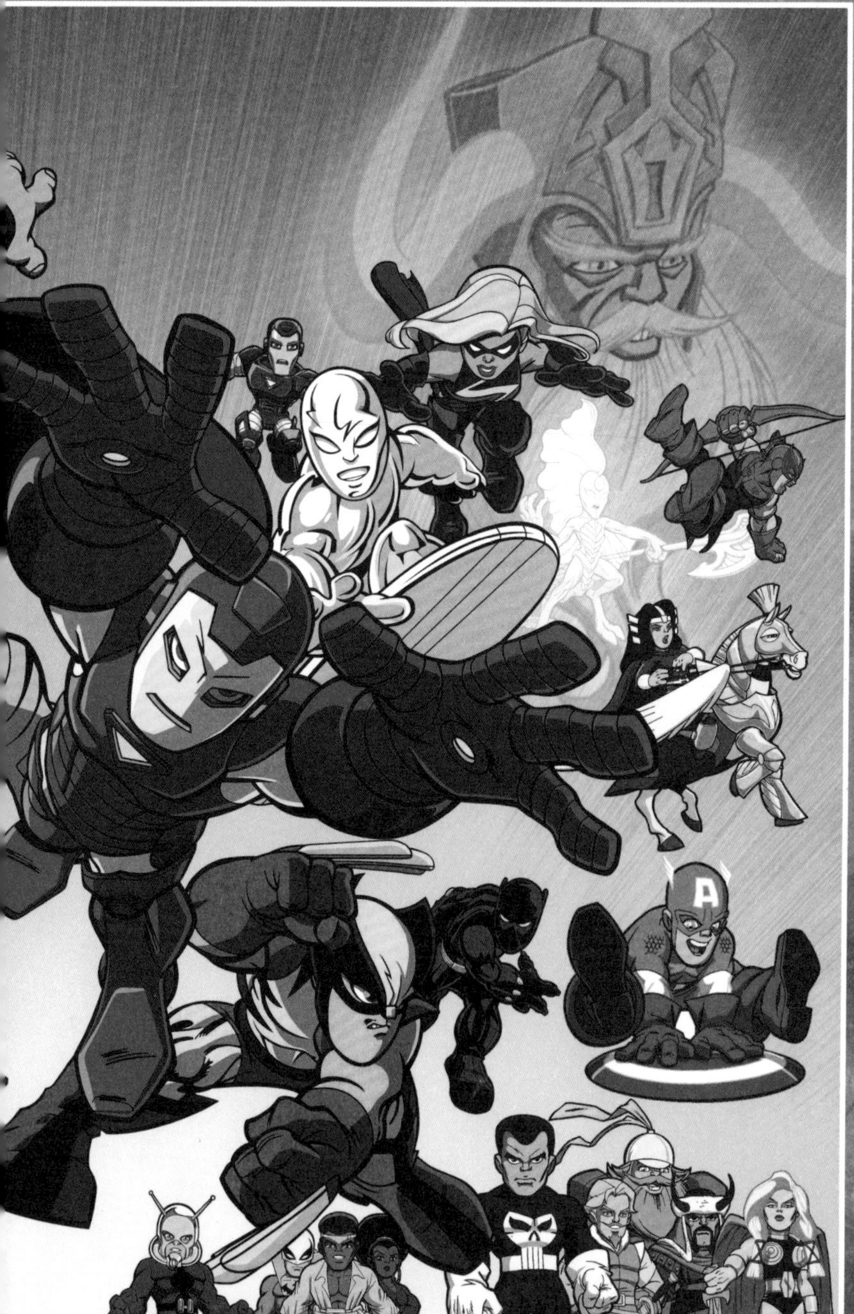

SUPER HERO SQUAD #1 VARIANT

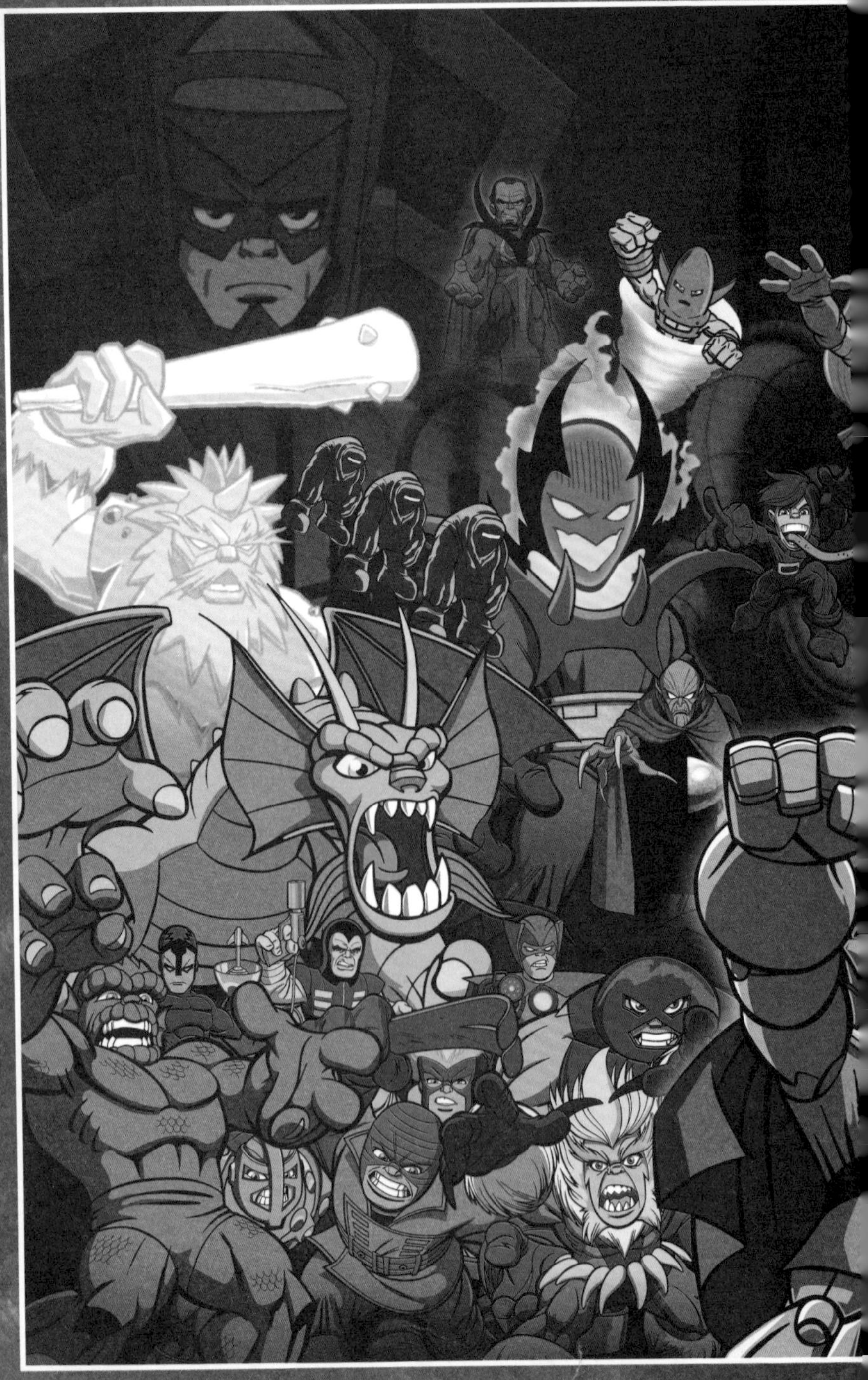

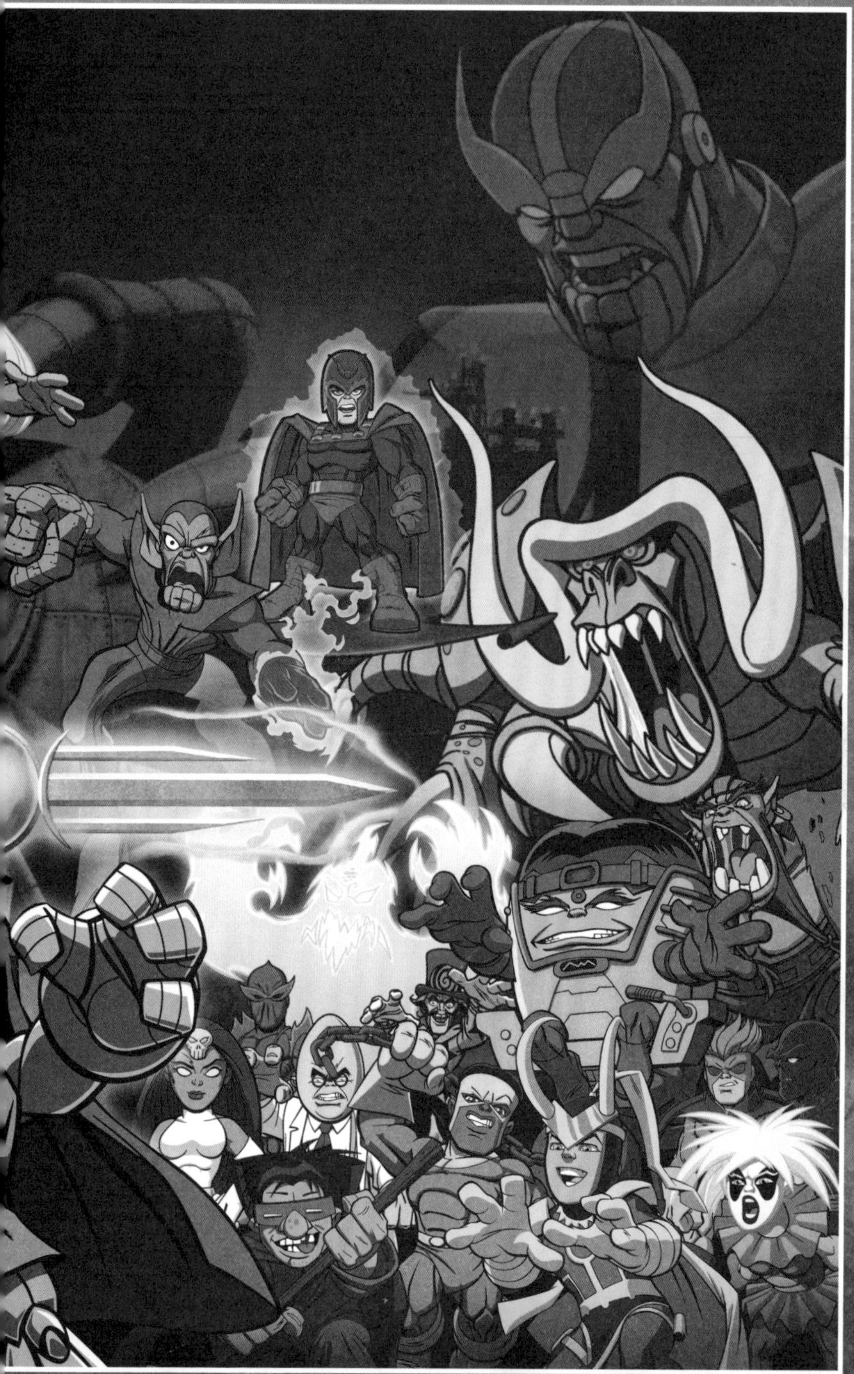

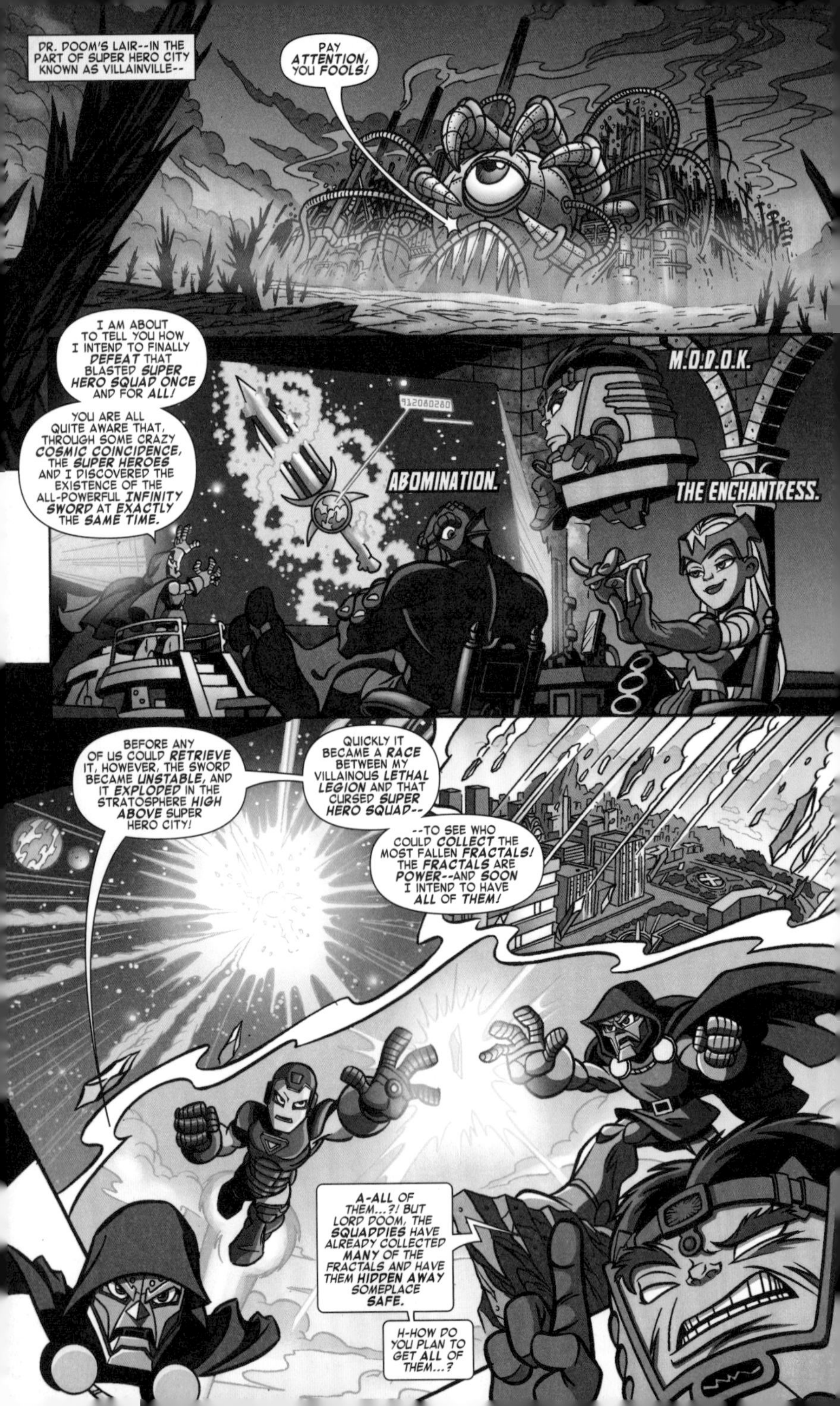

DR. DOOM'S LAIR--IN THE PART OF SUPER HERO CITY KNOWN AS VILLAINVILLE--
PAY ATTENTION, YOU FOOLS!
I AM ABOUT TO TELL YOU HOW I INTEND TO FINALLY DEFEAT THAT BLASTED SUPER HERO SQUAD ONCE AND FOR ALL!
YOU ARE ALL QUITE AWARE THAT, THROUGH SOME CRAZY COSMIC COINCIDENCE, THE SUPER HEROES AND I DISCOVERED THE EXISTENCE OF THE ALL-POWERFUL INFINITY SWORD AT EXACTLY THE SAME TIME.
M.O.D.O.K.
ABOMINATION.
THE ENCHANTRESS.
BEFORE ANY OF US COULD RETRIEVE IT, HOWEVER, THE SWORD BECAME UNSTABLE, AND IT EXPLODED IN THE STRATOSPHERE HIGH ABOVE SUPER HERO CITY!
QUICKLY IT BECAME A RACE BETWEEN MY VILLAINOUS LETHAL LEGION AND THAT CURSED SUPER HERO SQUAD--
--TO SEE WHO COULD COLLECT THE MOST FALLEN FRACTALS! THE FRACTALS ARE POWER--AND SOON I INTEND TO HAVE ALL OF THEM!
A-ALL OF THEM...?! BUT LORD DOOM, THE SQUADDIES HAVE ALREADY COLLECTED MANY OF THE FRACTALS AND HAVE THEM HIDDEN AWAY SOMEPLACE SAFE.
H-HOW DO YOU PLAN TO GET ALL OF THEM...?

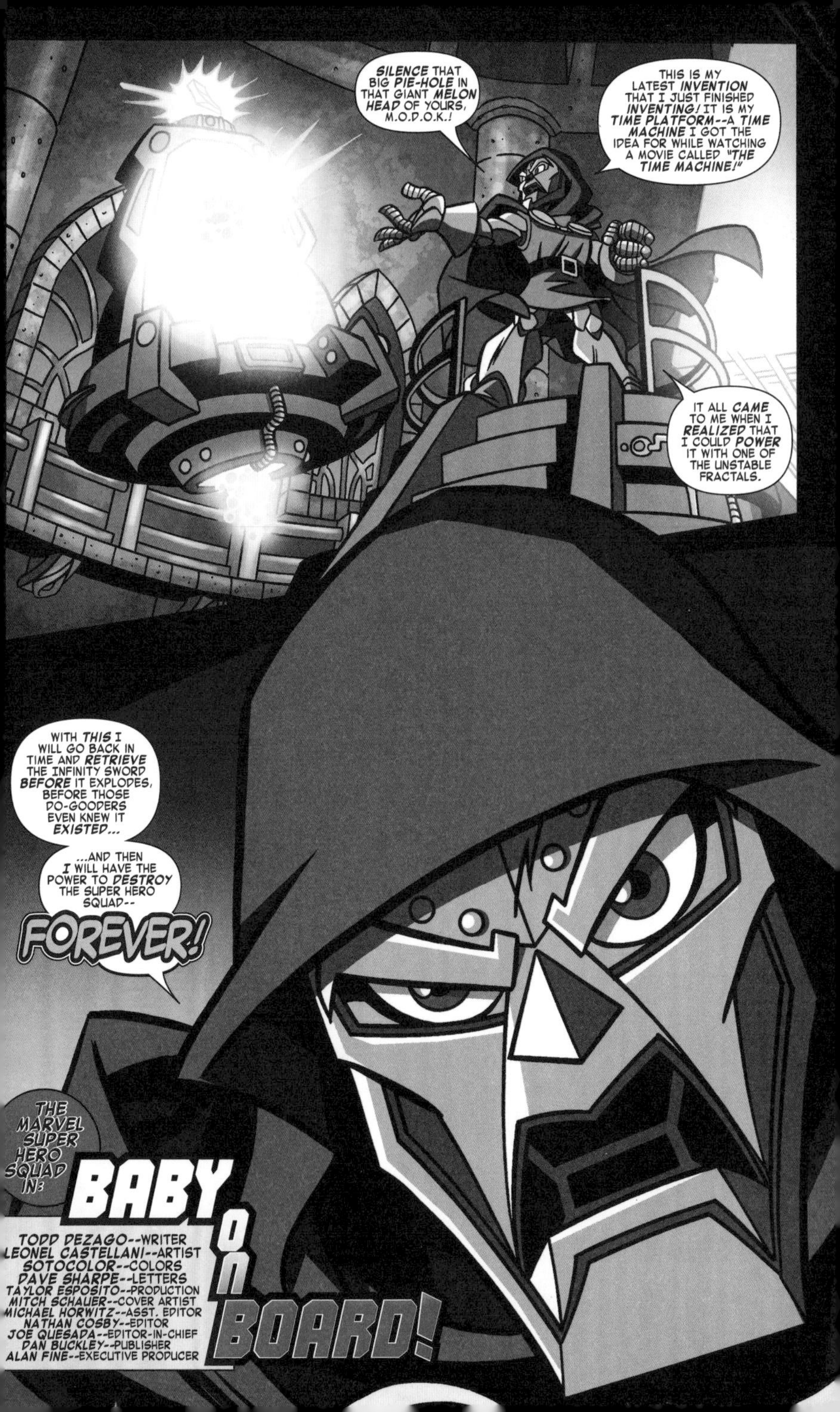
SILENCE THAT BIG PIE-HOLE IN THAT GIANT MELON HEAD OF YOURS, M.O.D.O.K.!
THIS IS MY LATEST INVENTION THAT I JUST FINISHED INVENTING! IT IS MY TIME PLATFORM--A TIME MACHINE I GOT THE IDEA FOR WHILE WATCHING A MOVIE CALLED "THE TIME MACHINE!"
IT ALL CAME TO ME WHEN I REALIZED THAT I COULD POWER IT WITH ONE OF THE UNSTABLE FRACTALS.
WITH THIS I WILL GO BACK IN TIME AND RETRIEVE THE INFINITY SWORD BEFORE IT EXPLODES, BEFORE THOSE DO-GOODERS EVEN KNEW IT EXISTED...
...AND THEN I WILL HAVE THE POWER TO DESTROY THE SUPER HERO SQUAD--
FOREVER!
THE MARVEL SUPER HERO SQUAD IN:
BABY ON BOARD!
TODD DEZAGO--WRITER
LEONEL CASTELLANI--ARTIST
SOTOCOLOR--COLORS
DAVE SHARPE--LETTERS
TAYLOR ESPOSITO--PRODUCTION
MITCH SCHAUER--COVER ARTIST
MICHAEL HORWITZ--ASST. EDITOR
NATHAN COSBY--EDITOR
JOE QUESADA--EDITOR-IN-CHIEF
DAN BUCKLEY--PUBLISHER
ALAN FINE--EXECUTIVE PRODUCER

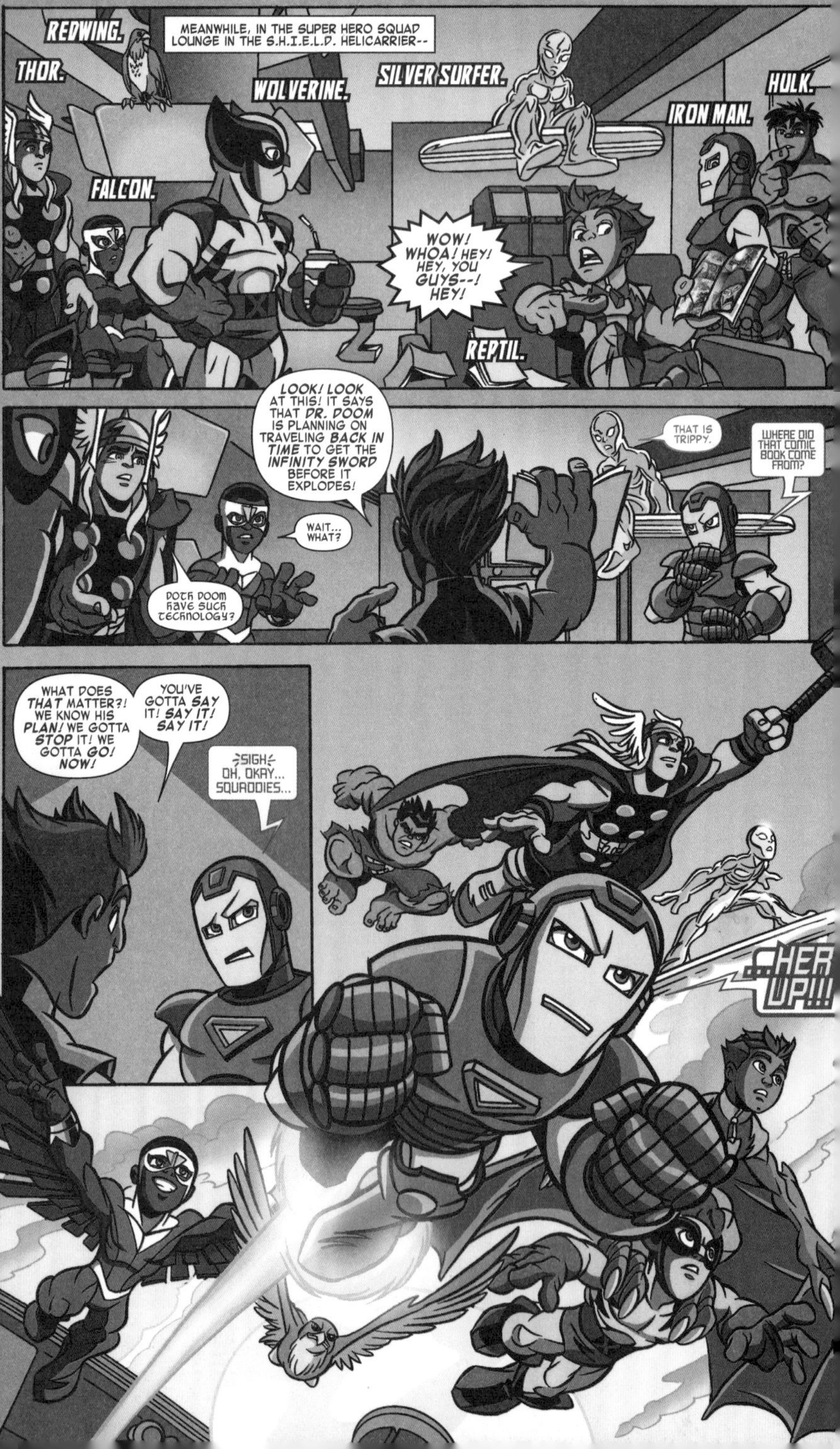
MEANWHILE, IN THE SUPER HERO SQUAD LOUNGE IN THE S.H.I.E.L.D. HELICARRIER--
REDWING.
THOR.
WOLVERINE.
SILVER SURFER.
HULK.
IRON MAN.
FALCON.
WOW! WHOA! HEY! HEY, YOU GUYS--! HEY!
REPTIL.
LOOK! LOOK AT THIS! IT SAYS THAT DR. DOOM IS PLANNING ON TRAVELING BACK IN TIME TO GET THE INFINITY SWORD BEFORE IT EXPLODES!
WAIT... WHAT?
DOTH DOOM HAVE SUCH TECHNOLOGY?
THAT IS TRIPPY.
WHERE DID THAT COMIC BOOK COME FROM?
WHAT DOES THAT MATTER?! WE KNOW HIS PLAN! WE GOTTA STOP IT! WE GOTTA GO! NOW!
YOU'VE GOTTA SAY IT! SAY IT! SAY IT!
SIGH OH, OKAY... SQUADDIES...
...HERO UP!!!

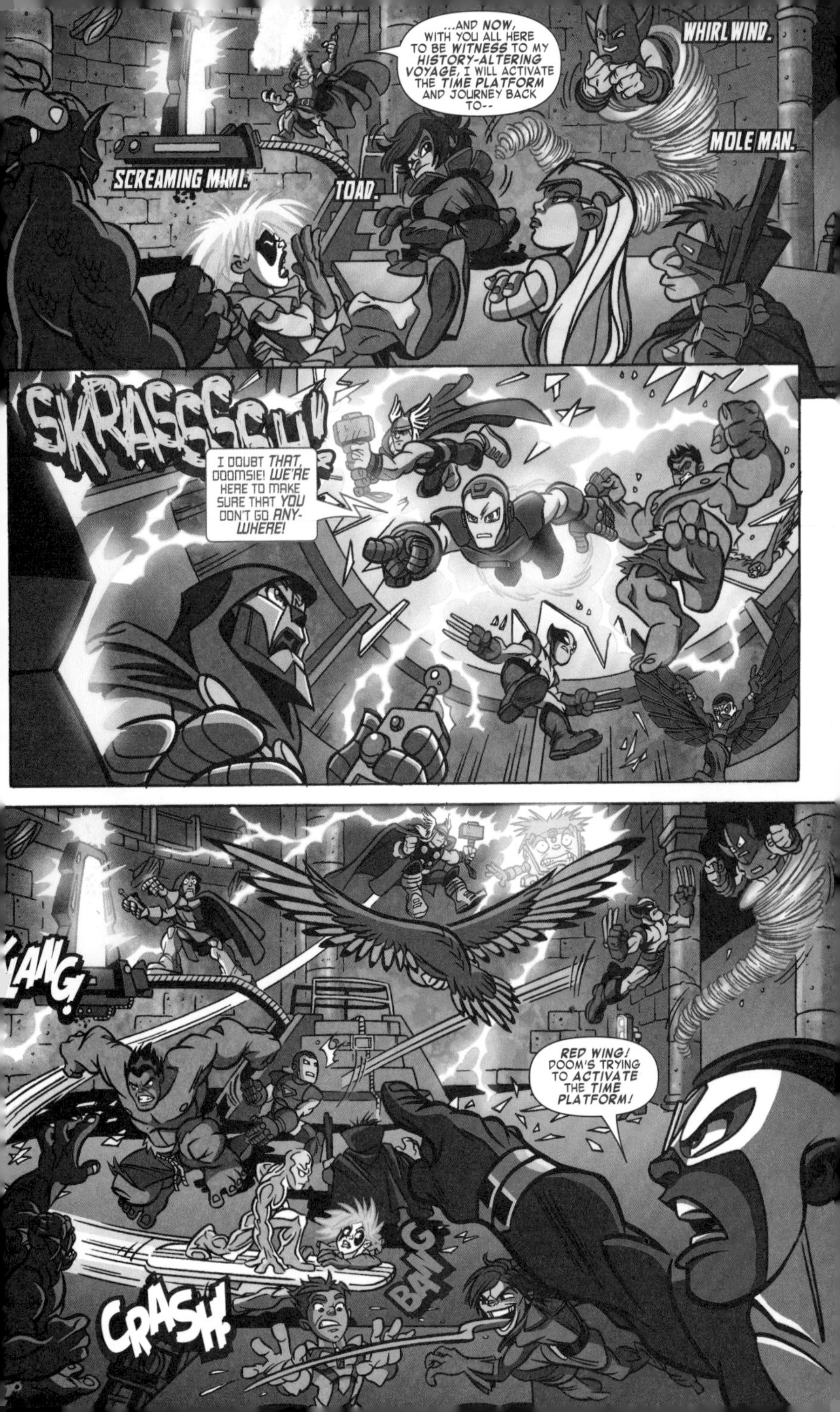
...AND NOW, WITH YOU ALL HERE TO BE WITNESS TO MY HISTORY-ALTERING VOYAGE, I WILL ACTIVATE THE TIME PLATFORM AND JOURNEY BACK TO--
WHIRLWIND.
SCREAMING MIMI.
TOAD.
MOLE MAN.
SKRASSSH!
I DOUBT THAT, DOOMSIE! WE'RE HERE TO MAKE SURE THAT YOU DON'T GO ANY-WHERE!
LANG!
RED WING! DOOM'S TRYING TO ACTIVATE THE TIME PLATFORM!
BANG
CRASH!

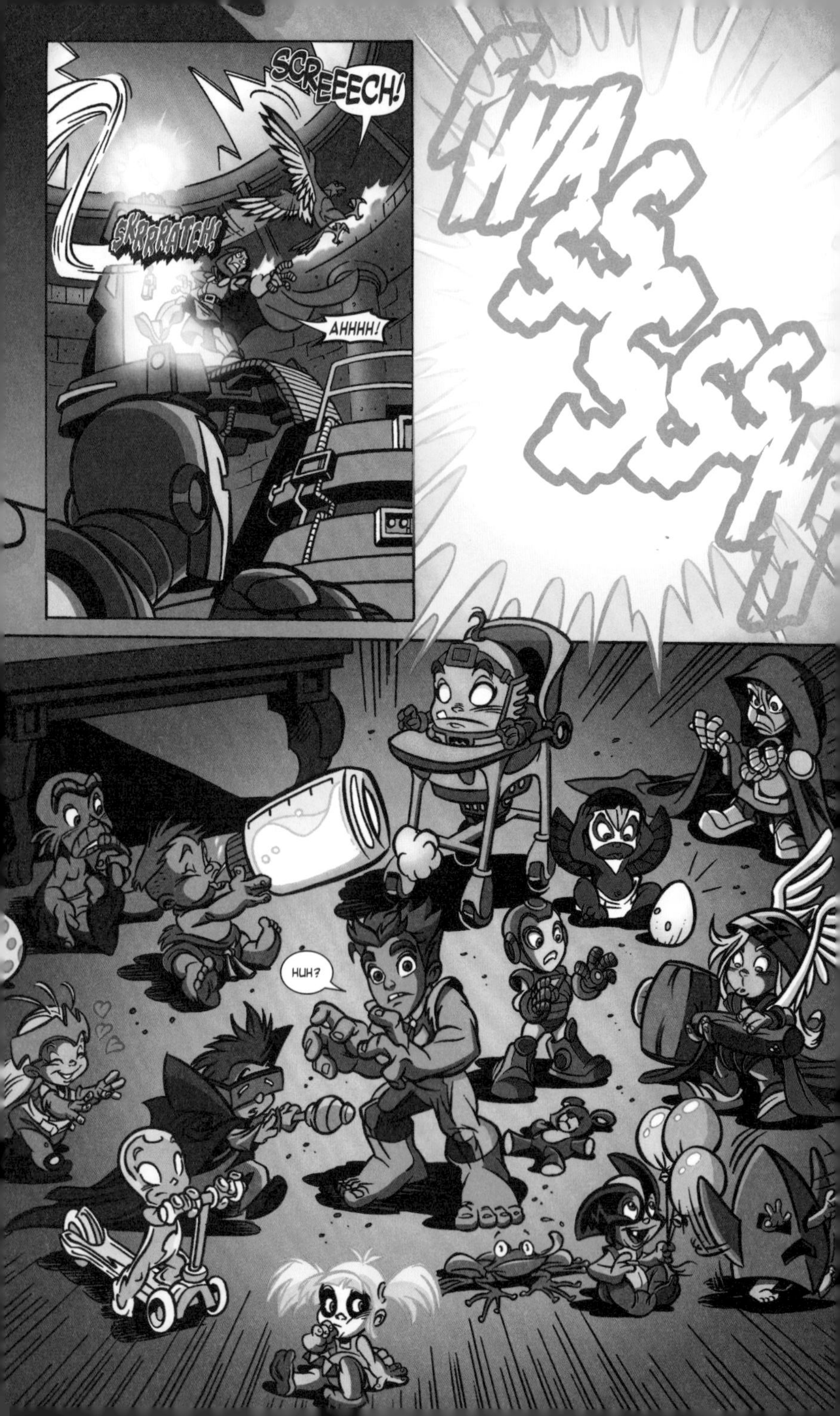
SCREEECH!
SKRRRATCH!
AHHHH!
WA-SSSH
HUH?

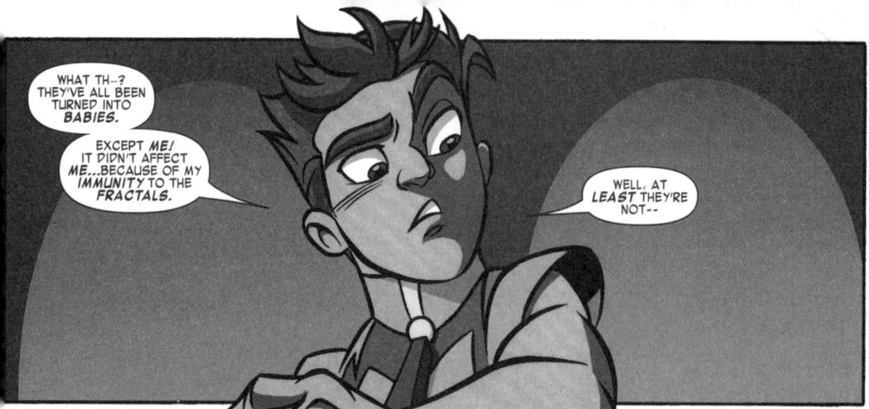
WHAT TH--? THEY'VE ALL BEEN TURNED INTO BABIES.
EXCEPT ME! IT DIDN'T AFFECT ME...BECAUSE OF MY IMMUNITY TO THE FRACTALS.
WELL, AT LEAST THEY'RE NOT--

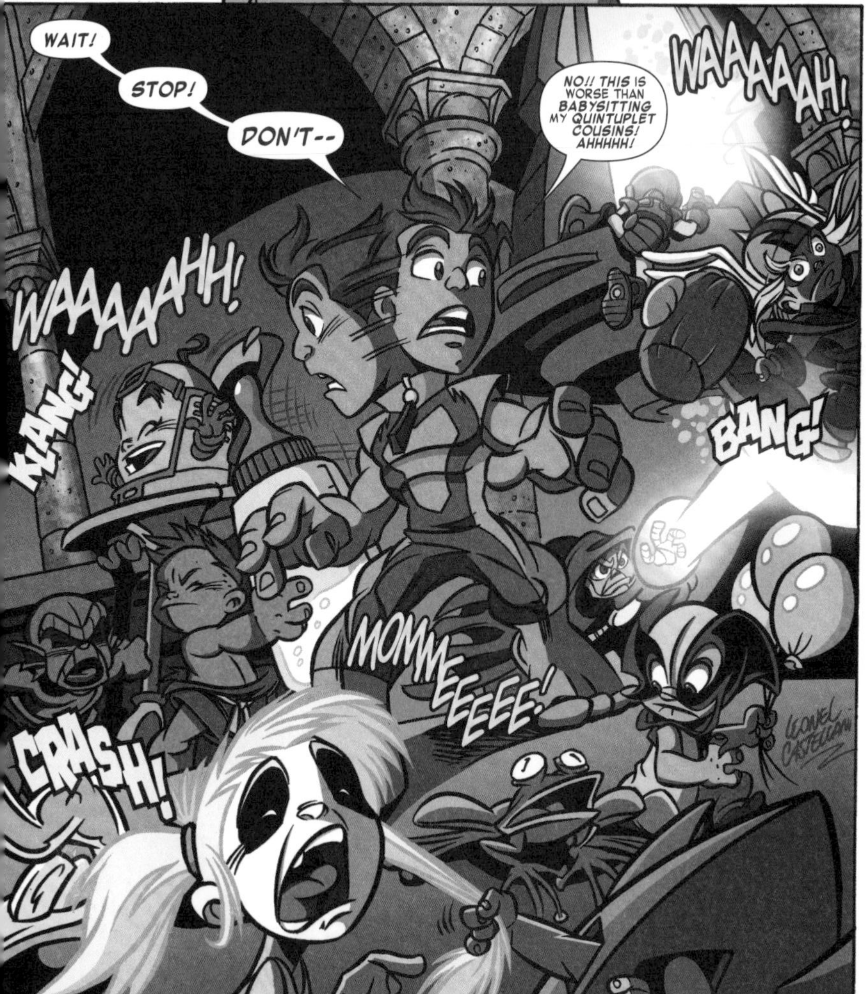
WAIT!
STOP!
DON'T--
NO!! THIS IS WORSE THAN BABYSITTING MY QUINTUPLET COUSINS! AHHHHH!
WAAAAAAH!
WAAAAAAHH!
KLANG!
BANG!
MOMMEEEEEE!
CRASH!
LEONEL CASTELLANI

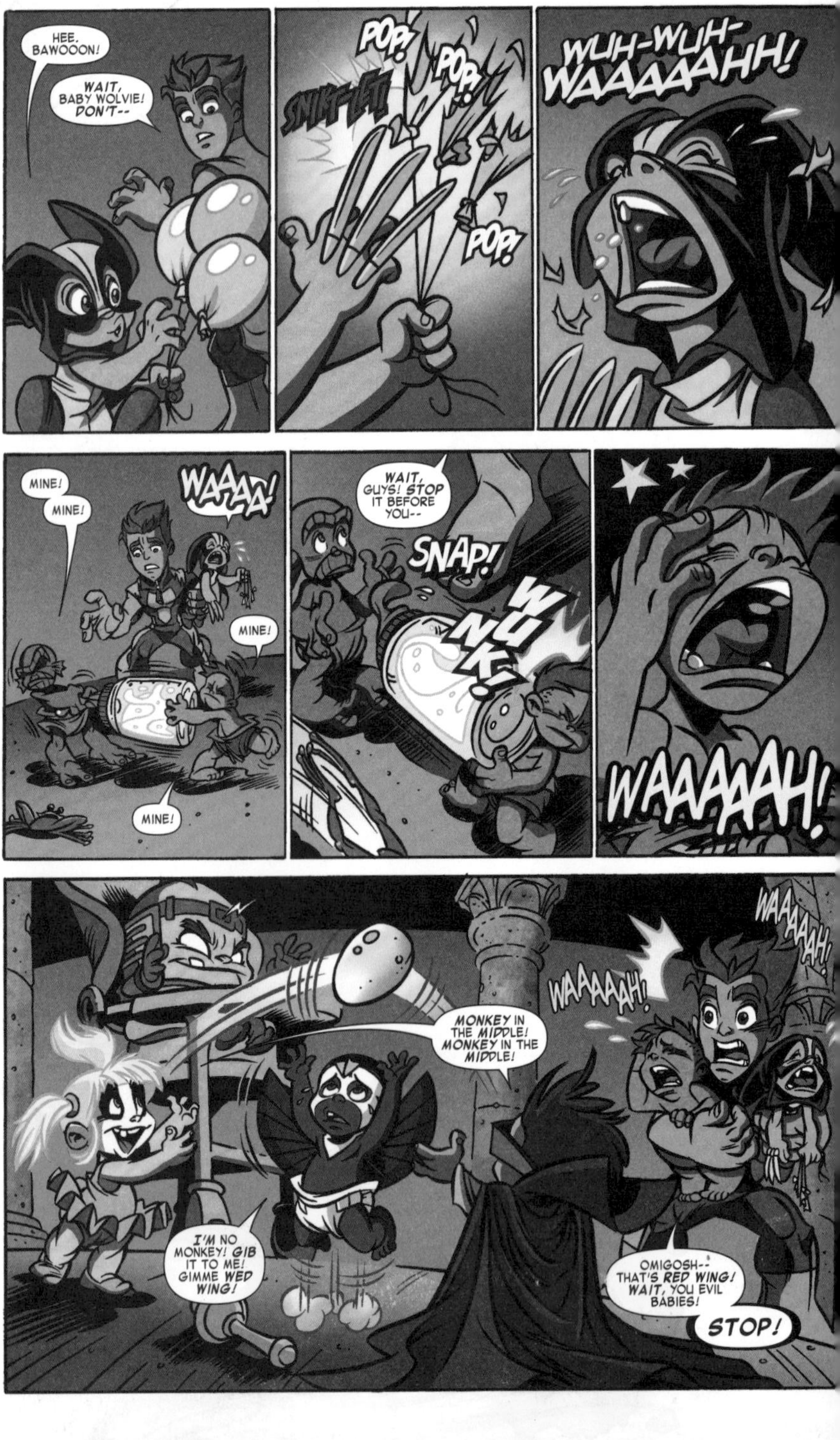

HEE. BAWOOON!
WAIT, BABY WOLVIE! DON'T--
SNIKT-LETT
POP!
POP!
POP!
WUH-WUH-WAAAAAHH!
MINE!
MINE!
WAAAA!
MINE!
MINE!
WAIT, GUYS! STOP IT BEFORE YOU--
SNAP!
WUNK!
WAAAAAH!
WAAAAAH!
WAAAAAH!
MONKEY IN THE MIDDLE! MONKEY IN THE MIDDLE!
I'M NO MONKEY! GIB IT TO ME! GIMME WED WING!
OMIGOSH-- THAT'S RED WING! WAIT, YOU EVIL BABIES!
STOP!

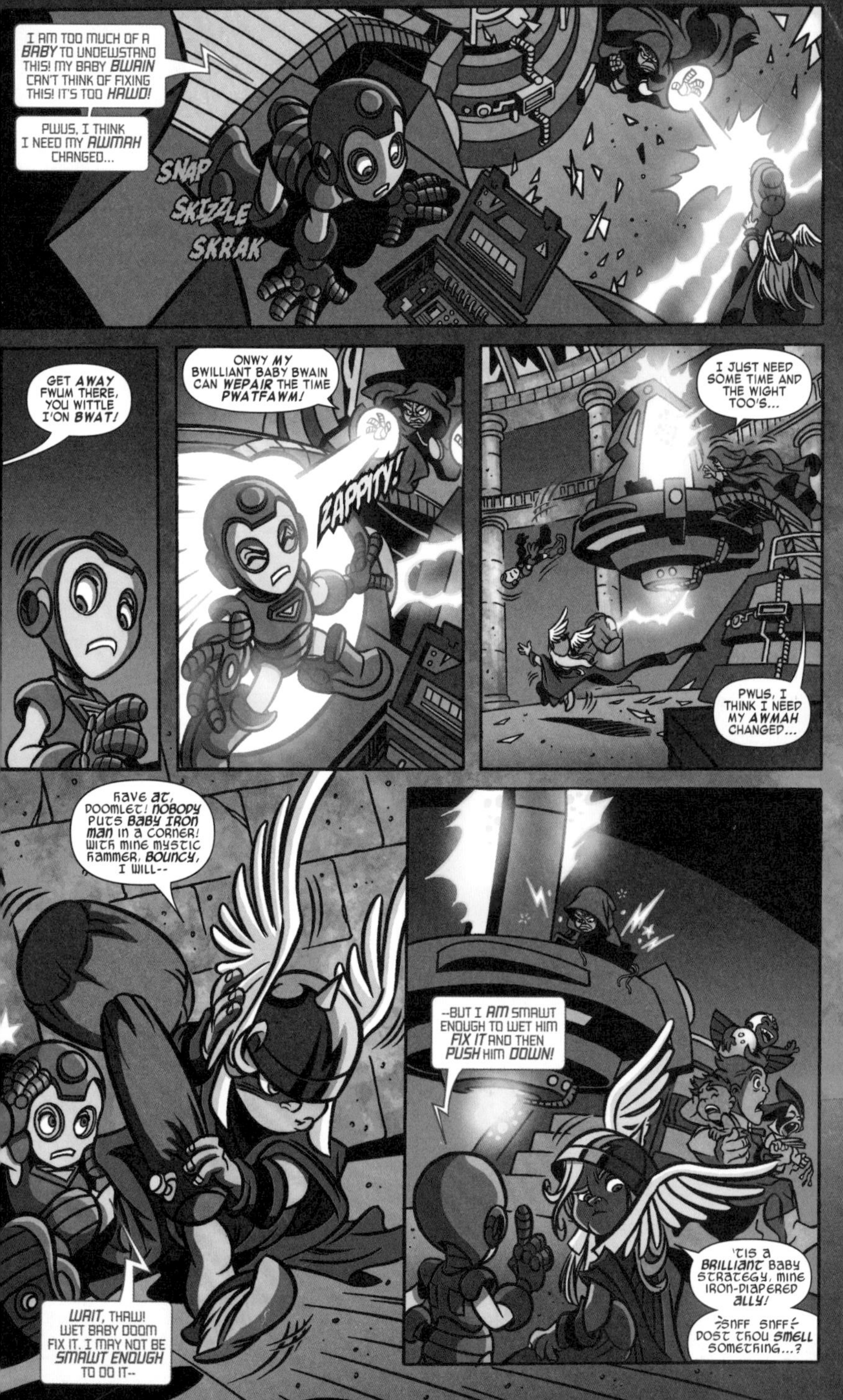

I AM TOO MUCH OF A BABY TO UNDEWSTAND THIS! MY BABY BWAIN CAN'T THINK OF FIXING THIS! IT'S TOO HAWD!
PWUS, I THINK I NEED MY AWMAH CHANGED...
SNAP
SKIZZLE
SKRAK
GET AWAY FWUM THERE, YOU WITTLE I'ON BWAT!
ONWY MY BWILLIANT BABY BWAIN CAN WEPAIR THE TIME PWATFAWM!
ZAPPITY!
I JUST NEED SOME TIME AND THE WIGHT TOO'S...
PWUS, I THINK I NEED MY AWMAH CHANGED...
HAVE AT, DOOMLET! NOBODY PUTS BABY IRON MAN IN A CORNER! WITH MINE MYSTIC HAMMER, BOUNCY, I WILL--
WAIT, THAW! WET BABY DOOM FIX IT. I MAY NOT BE SMAWT ENOUGH TO DO IT--
--BUT I AM SMAWT ENOUGH TO WET HIM FIX IT AND THEN PUSH HIM DOWN!
'TIS A BRILLIANT BABY STRATEGY, MINE IRON-DIAPERED ALLY!
SNFF SNFF DOST THOU SMELL SOMETHING...?

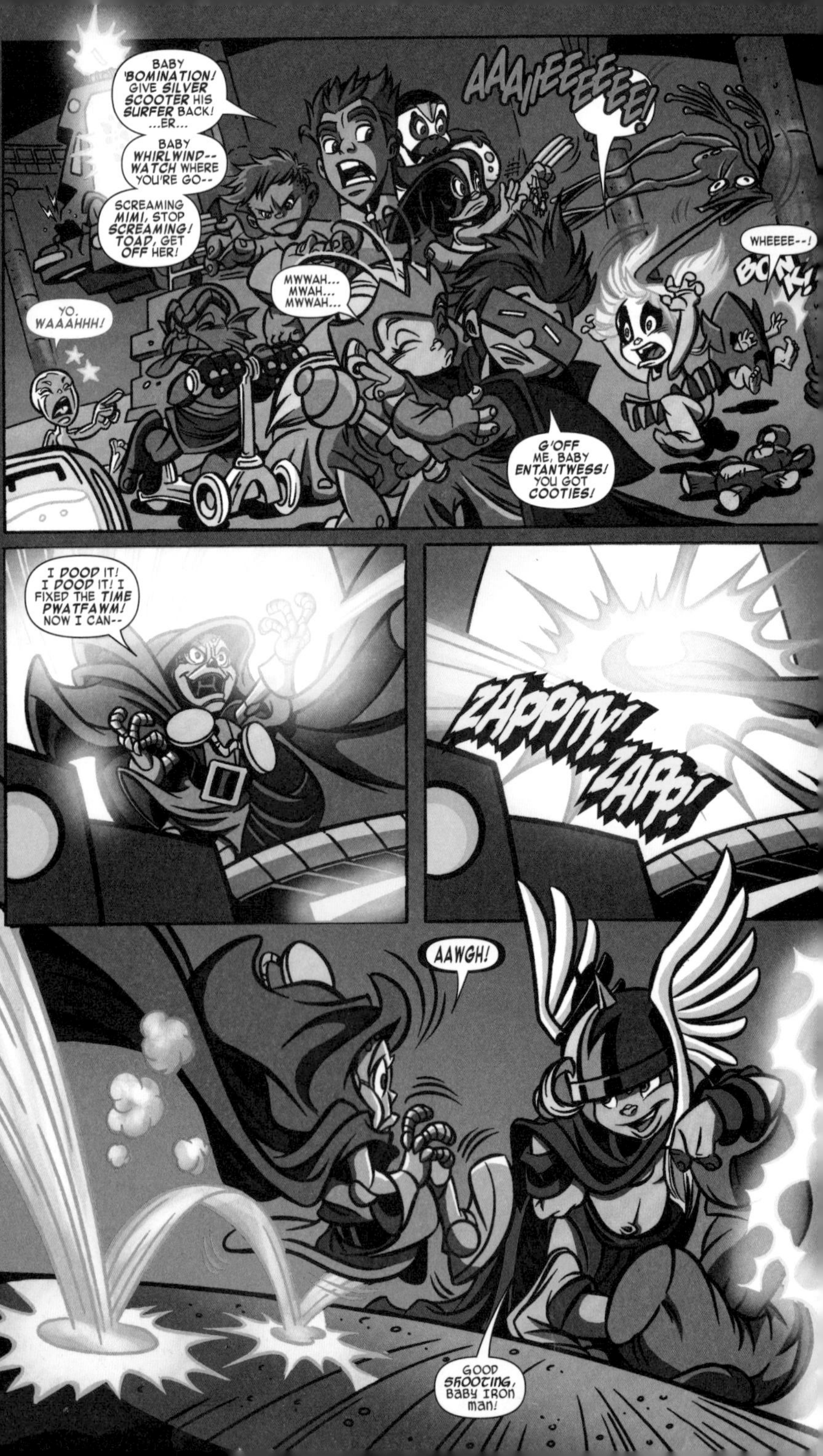
BABY 'BOMINATION! GIVE SILVER SCOOTER HIS SURFER BACK! ...ER...
BABY WHIRLWIND-- WATCH WHERE YOU'RE GO--
SCREAMING MIMI, STOP SCREAMING! TOAD, GET OFF HER!
AAAIIEEEEEEE!
YO. WAAAHHH!
MWWAH... MWAH... MWWAH...
WHEEEE--!
BONK!
G'OFF ME, BABY ENTANTWESS! YOU GOT COOTIES!
I DOOD IT! I DOOD IT! I FIXED THE TIME PWATFAWM! NOW I CAN--
ZAPPITY! ZAPP!
AAWGH!
GOOD SHOOTING, BABY IRON MAN!

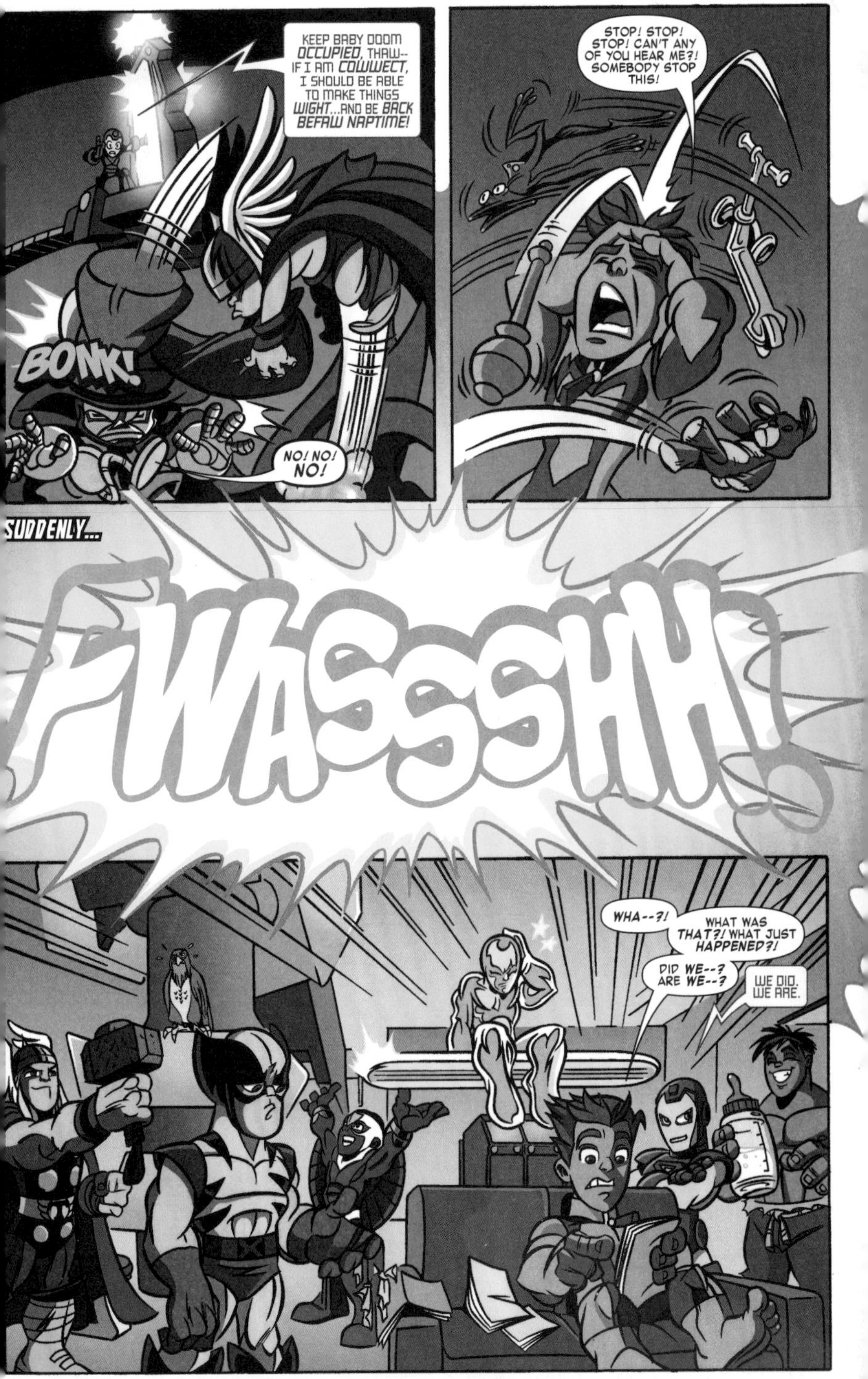
KEEP BABY DOOM OCCUPIED, THAW-- IF I AM COWWECT, I SHOULD BE ABLE TO MAKE THINGS WIGHT...AND BE BACK BEFAW NAPTIME!
BONK!
NO! NO! NO!
STOP! STOP! STOP! CAN'T ANY OF YOU HEAR ME?! SOMEBODY STOP THIS!
SUDDENLY...
PWASSSHH!
WHA--?!
WHAT WAS THAT?! WHAT JUST HAPPENED?!
DID WE--? ARE WE--?
WE DID. WE ARE.

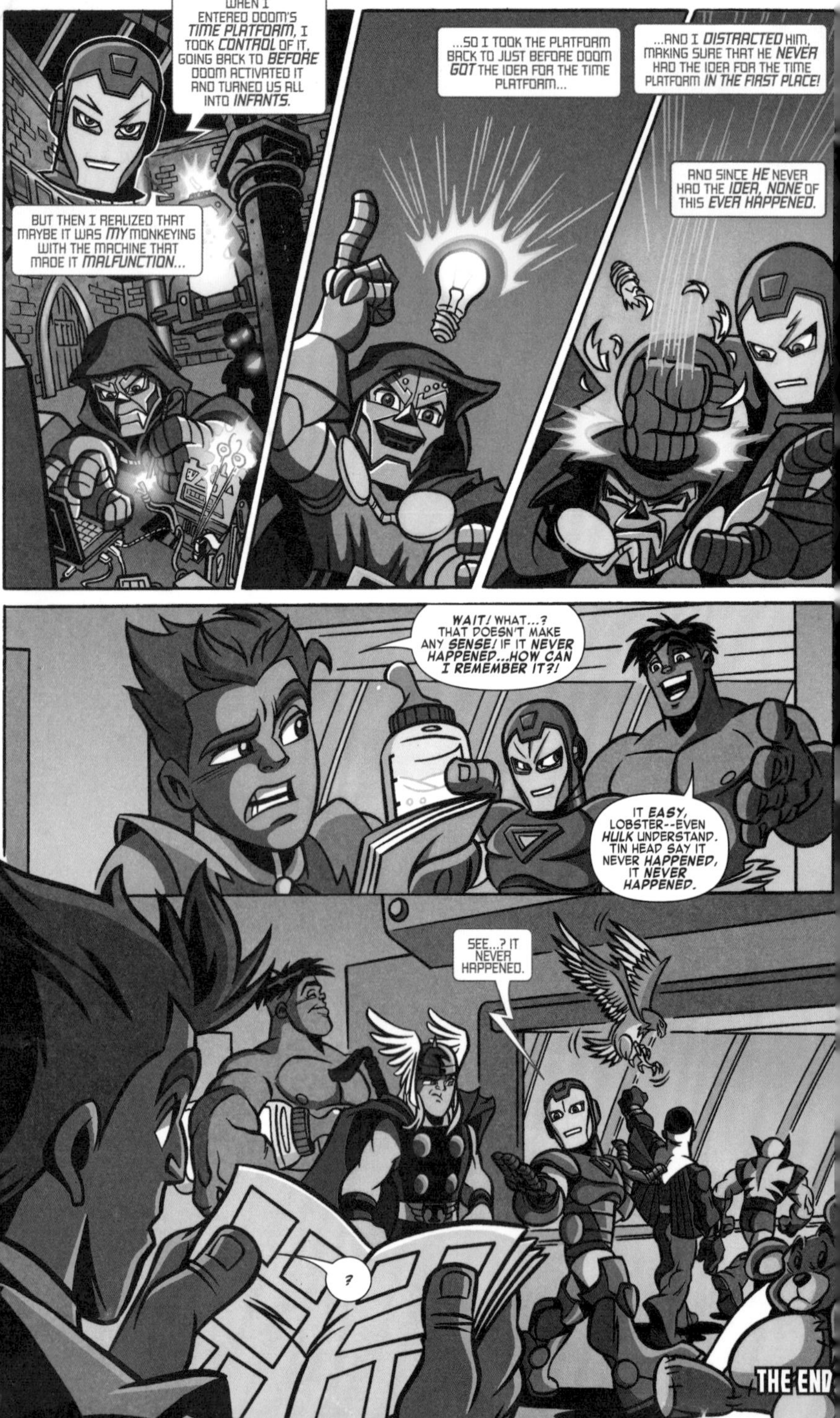
WHEN I ENTERED DOOM'S TIME PLATFORM, I TOOK CONTROL OF IT, GOING BACK TO BEFORE DOOM ACTIVATED IT AND TURNED US ALL INTO INFANTS.
BUT THEN I REALIZED THAT MAYBE IT WAS MY MONKEYING WITH THE MACHINE THAT MADE IT MALFUNCTION...
...SO I TOOK THE PLATFORM BACK TO JUST BEFORE DOOM GOT THE IDEA FOR THE TIME PLATFORM...
...AND I DISTRACTED HIM, MAKING SURE THAT HE NEVER HAD THE IDEA FOR THE TIME PLATFORM IN THE FIRST PLACE!
AND SINCE HE NEVER HAD THE IDEA, NONE OF THIS EVER HAPPENED.
WAIT! WHAT...? THAT DOESN'T MAKE ANY SENSE! IF IT NEVER HAPPENED...HOW CAN I REMEMBER IT?!
IT EASY, LOBSTER--EVEN HULK UNDERSTAND. TIN HEAD SAY IT NEVER HAPPENED, IT NEVER HAPPENED.
SEE...? IT NEVER HAPPENED.
?
THE END

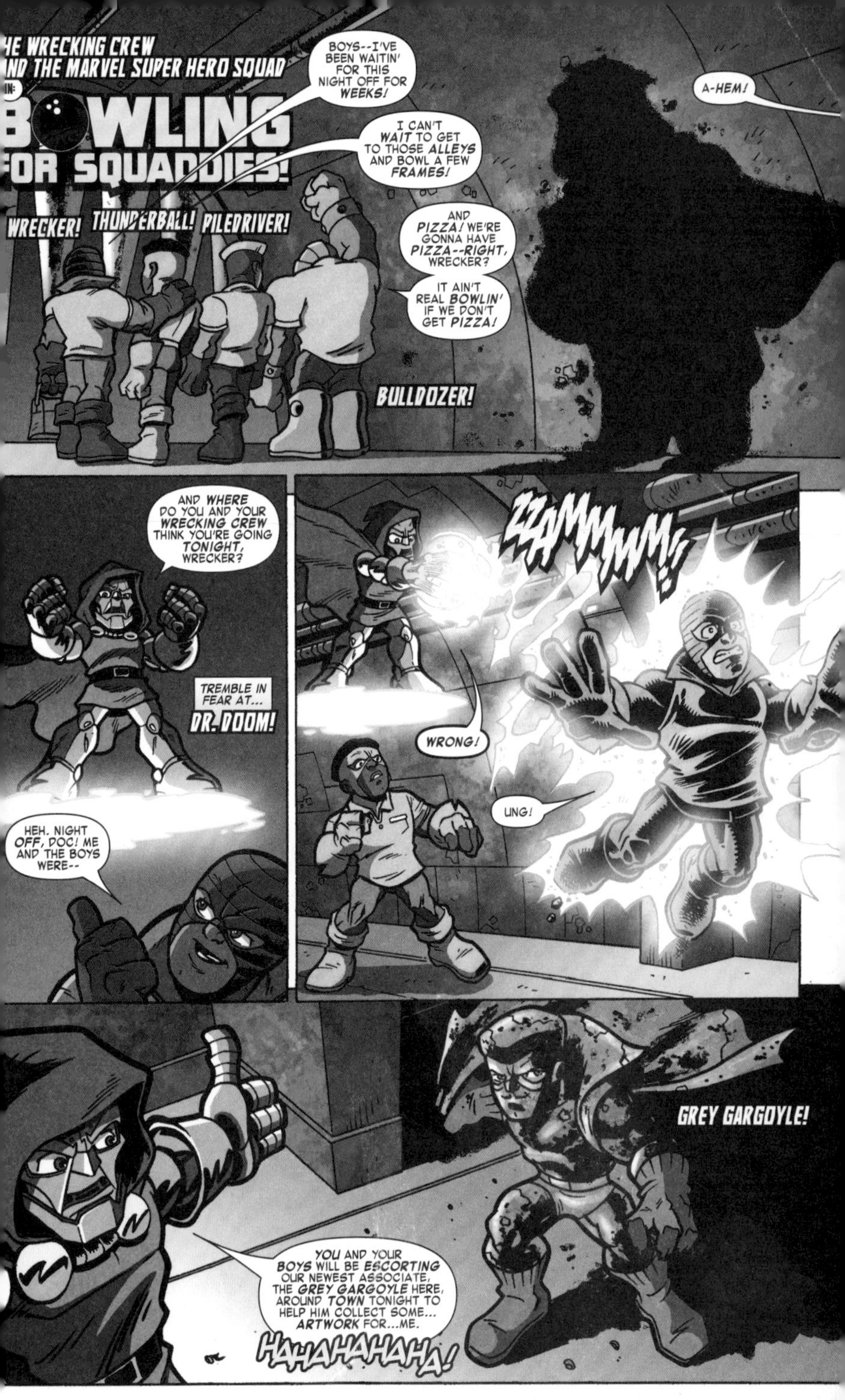

HE WRECKING CREW
ND THE MARVEL SUPER HERO SQUAD
IN:
BOWLING FOR SQUADDIES!
BOYS--I'VE BEEN WAITIN' FOR THIS NIGHT OFF FOR WEEKS!
I CAN'T WAIT TO GET TO THOSE ALLEYS AND BOWL A FEW FRAMES!
WRECKER! THUNDERBALL! PILEDRIVER!
AND PIZZA! WE'RE GONNA HAVE PIZZA--RIGHT, WRECKER?
IT AIN'T REAL BOWLIN' IF WE DON'T GET PIZZA!
BULLDOZER!
A-HEM!
AND WHERE DO YOU AND YOUR WRECKING CREW THINK YOU'RE GOING TONIGHT, WRECKER?
TREMBLE IN FEAR AT... DR. DOOM!
HEH. NIGHT OFF, DOC! ME AND THE BOYS WERE--
ZZAMMMMM!
WRONG!
UNG!
GREY GARGOYLE!
YOU AND YOUR BOYS WILL BE ESCORTING OUR NEWEST ASSOCIATE, THE GREY GARGOYLE HERE, AROUND TOWN TONIGHT TO HELP HIM COLLECT SOME... ARTWORK FOR...ME.
HAHAHAHAHAHA!

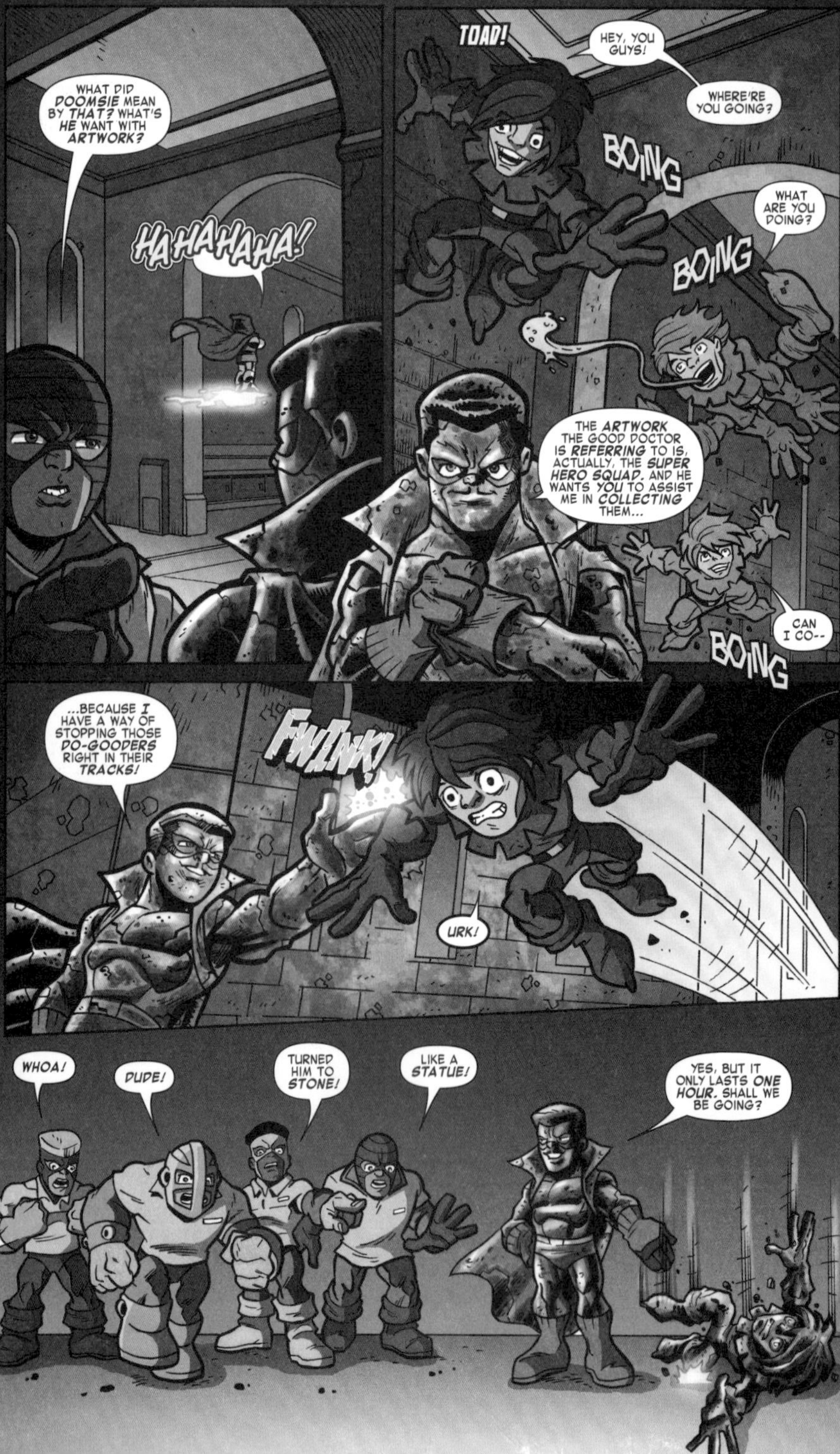
WHAT DID DOOMSIE MEAN BY THAT? WHAT'S HE WANT WITH ARTWORK?
HAHAHAHA!
TOAD!
HEY, YOU GUYS!
WHERE'RE YOU GOING?
BOING
WHAT ARE YOU DOING?
BOING
THE ARTWORK THE GOOD DOCTOR IS REFERRING TO IS, ACTUALLY, THE SUPER HERO SQUAD. AND HE WANTS YOU TO ASSIST ME IN COLLECTING THEM...
CAN I CO--
BOING
...BECAUSE I HAVE A WAY OF STOPPING THOSE DO-GOODERS RIGHT IN THEIR TRACKS!
FWINK!
URK!
WHOA!
DUDE!
TURNED HIM TO STONE!
LIKE A STATUE!
YES, BUT IT ONLY LASTS ONE HOUR. SHALL WE BE GOING?

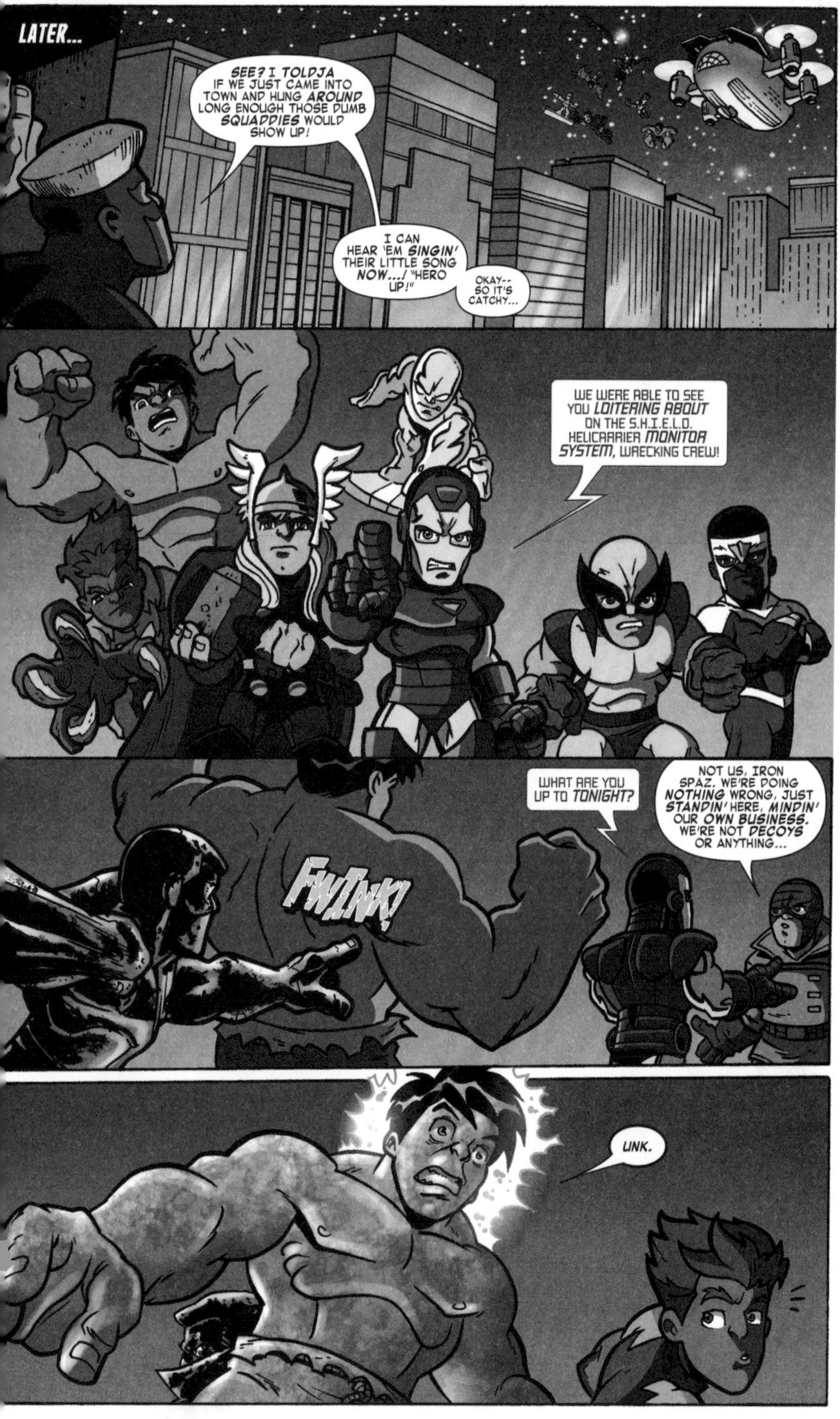
LATER...
SEE? I TOLDJA IF WE JUST CAME INTO TOWN AND HUNG AROUND LONG ENOUGH THOSE DUMB SQUADDIES WOULD SHOW UP!
I CAN HEAR 'EM SINGIN' THEIR LITTLE SONG NOW...! "HERO UP!"
OKAY-- SO IT'S CATCHY...
WE WERE ABLE TO SEE YOU LOITERING ABOUT ON THE S.H.I.E.L.D. HELICARRIER MONITOR SYSTEM, WRECKING CREW!
WHAT ARE YOU UP TO TONIGHT?
NOT US, IRON SPAZ. WE'RE DOING NOTHING WRONG, JUST STANDIN' HERE, MINDIN' OUR OWN BUSINESS. WE'RE NOT DECOYS OR ANYTHING...
FWINK!
UNK.

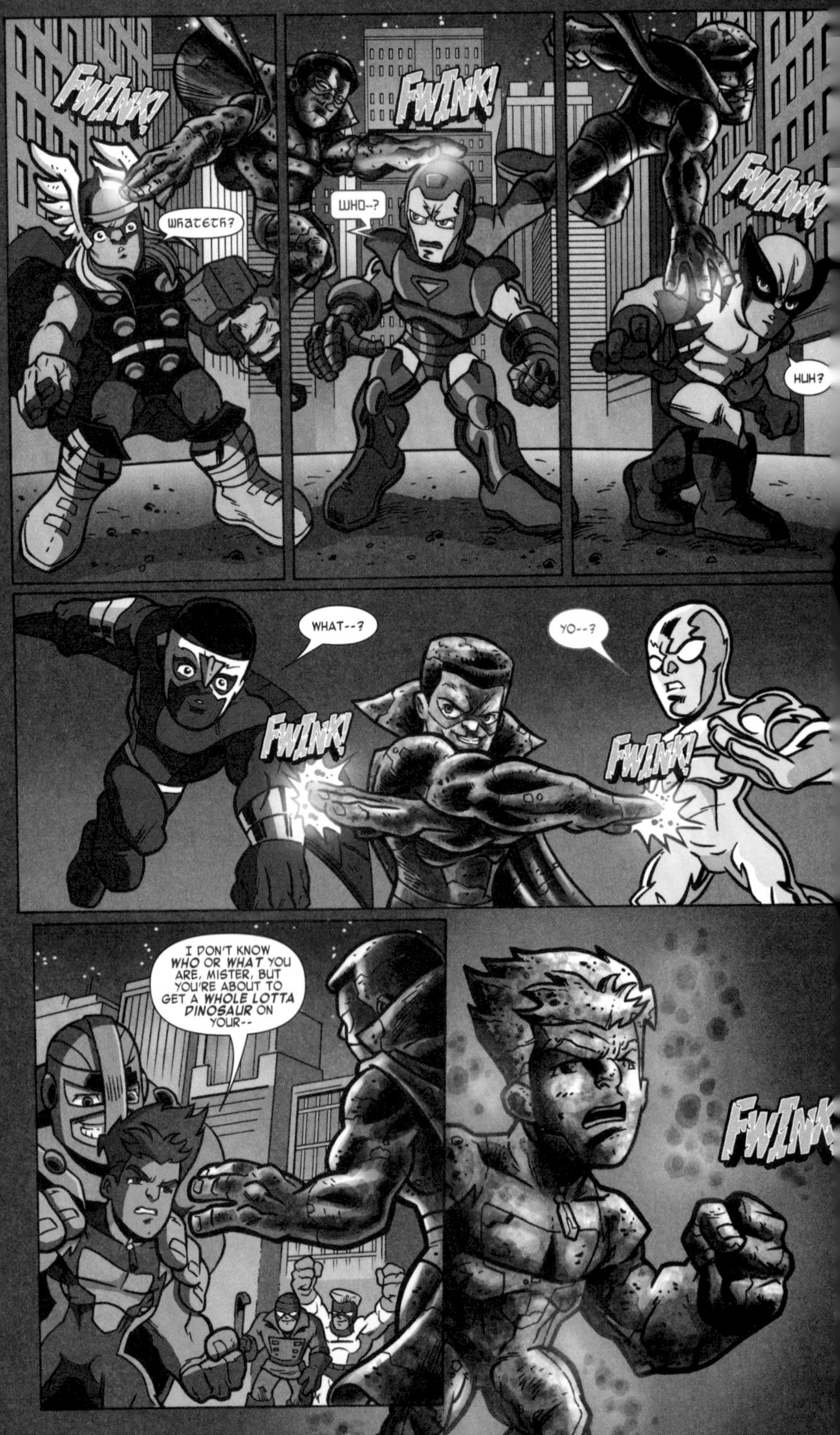
FWINK!
WHATETH?
FWINK!
WHO--?
FWINK!
HUH?
WHAT--?
YO--?
FWINK!
FWINK!
I DON'T KNOW WHO OR WHAT YOU ARE, MISTER, BUT YOU'RE ABOUT TO GET A WHOLE LOTTA DINOSAUR ON YOUR--
FWINK

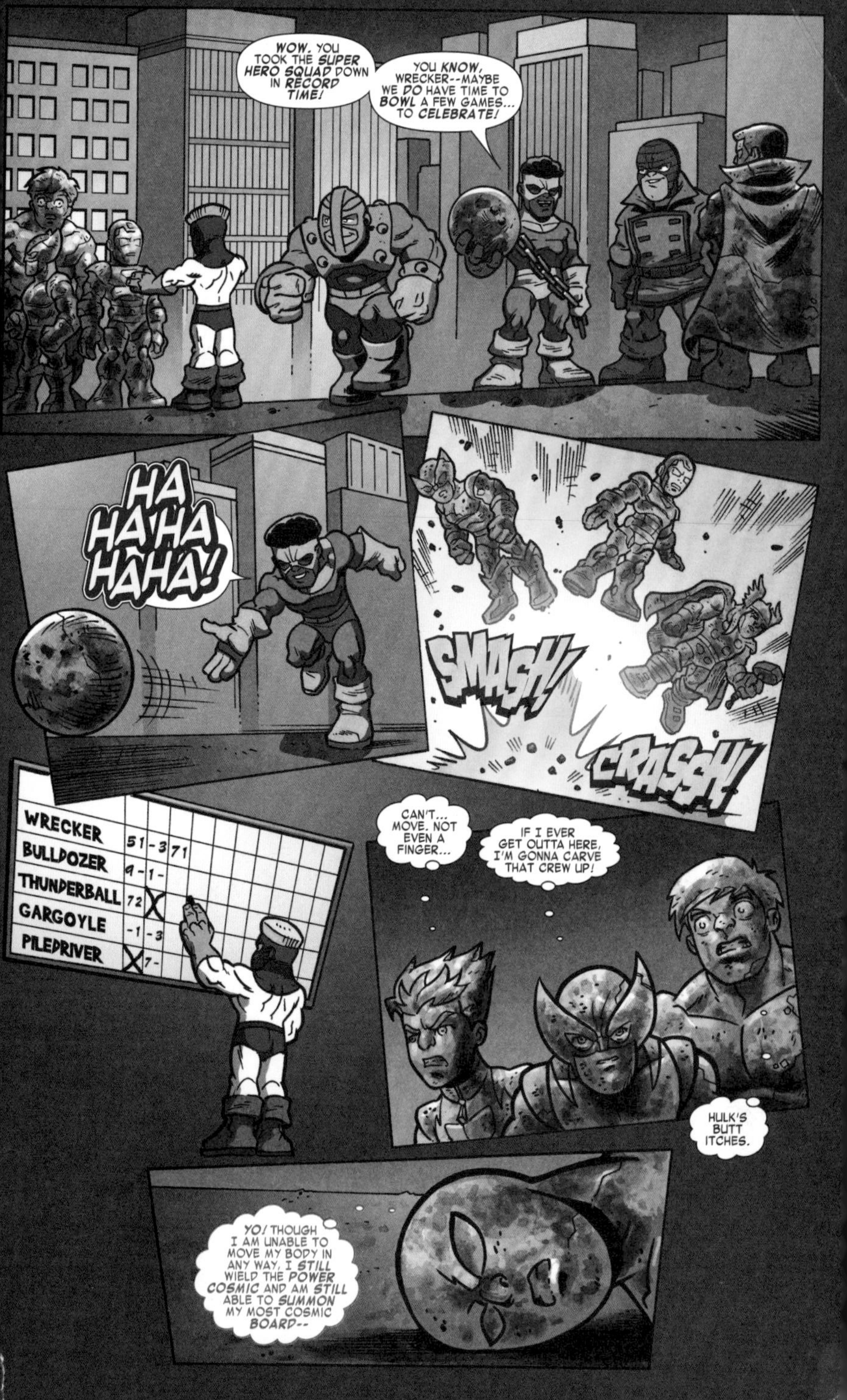
WOW. YOU TOOK THE SUPER HERO SQUAD DOWN IN RECORD TIME!
YOU KNOW, WRECKER--MAYBE WE DO HAVE TIME TO BOWL A FEW GAMES... TO CELEBRATE!
HA HA HA HA HA!
SMASH!
CRASSH!
WRECKER 51 - 3 71
BULLDOZER 9 - 1 -
THUNDERBALL 72 X
GARGOYLE - 1 - 3
PILEDRIVER X 7 -
CAN'T... MOVE. NOT EVEN A FINGER...
IF I EVER GET OUTTA HERE, I'M GONNA CARVE THAT CREW UP!
HULK'S BUTT ITCHES.
YO! THOUGH I AM UNABLE TO MOVE MY BODY IN ANY WAY, I STILL WIELD THE POWER COSMIC AND AM STILL ABLE TO SUMMON MY MOST COSMIC BOARD--

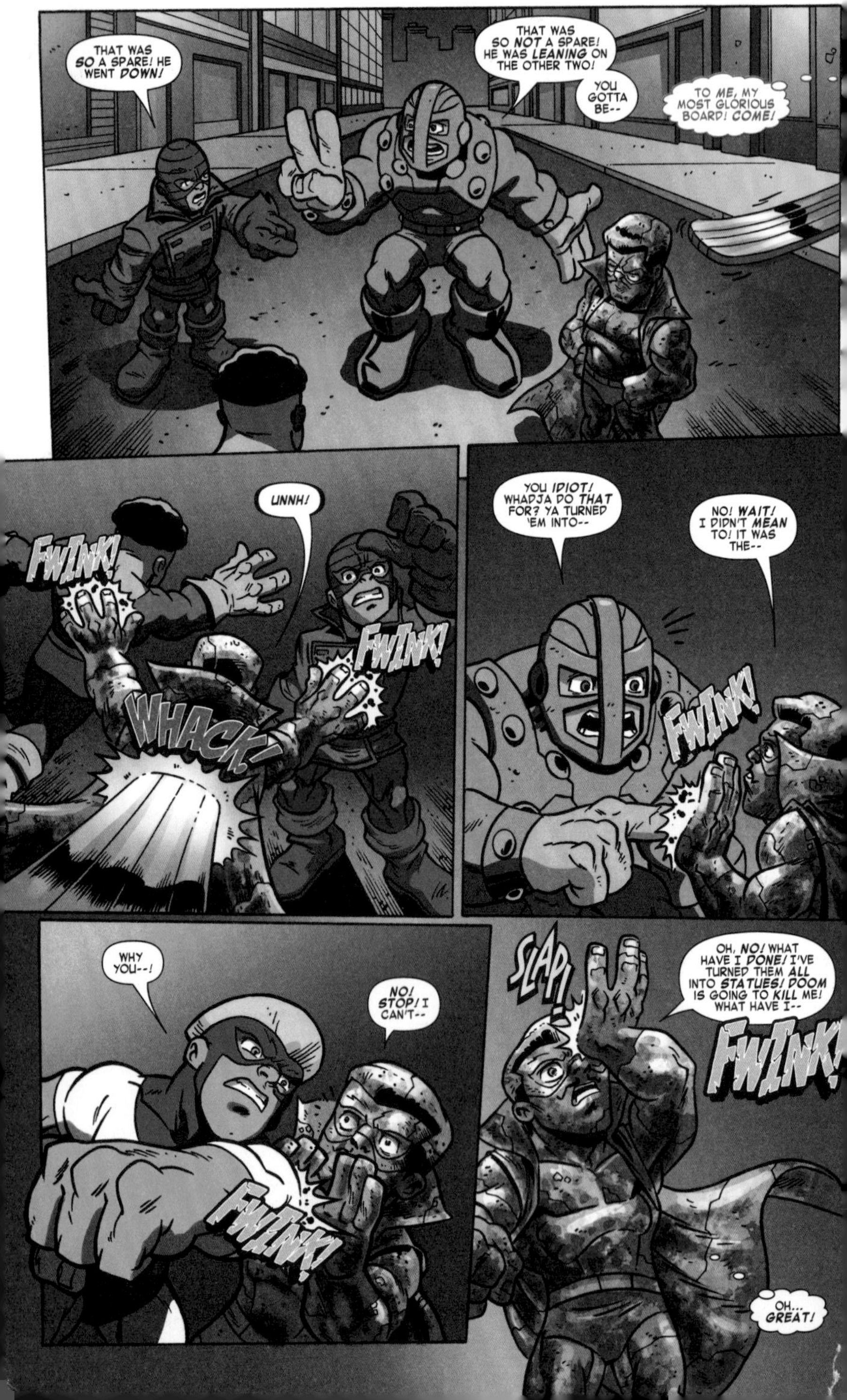
THAT WAS SO A SPARE! HE WENT DOWN!
THAT WAS SO NOT A SPARE! HE WAS LEANING ON THE OTHER TWO!
YOU GOTTA BE--
TO ME, MY MOST GLORIOUS BOARD! COME!
FWINK!
UNNH!
FWINK!
WHACK!
YOU IDIOT! WHADJA DO THAT FOR? YA TURNED 'EM INTO--
NO! WAIT! I DIDN'T MEAN TO! IT WAS THE--
FWINK!
WHY YOU--!
NO! STOP! I CAN'T--
FWINK!
SLAP!
OH, NO! WHAT HAVE I DONE! I'VE TURNED THEM ALL INTO STATUES! DOOM IS GOING TO KILL ME! WHAT HAVE I--
FWINK!
OH... GREAT!

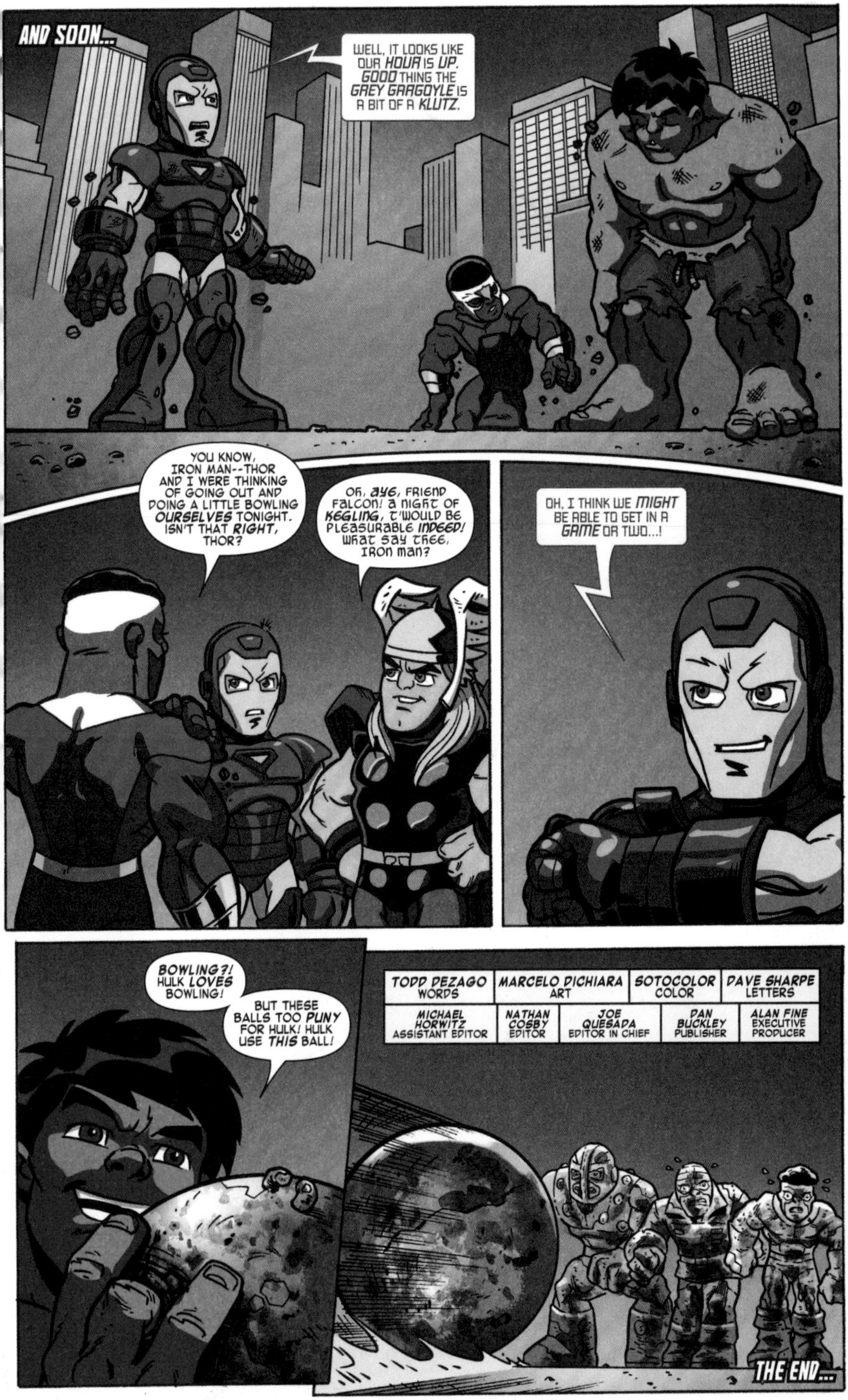
AND SOON...
WELL, IT LOOKS LIKE OUR HOUR IS UP. GOOD THING THE GREY GARGOYLE IS A BIT OF A KLUTZ.
YOU KNOW, IRON MAN--THOR AND I WERE THINKING OF GOING OUT AND DOING A LITTLE BOWLING OURSELVES TONIGHT. ISN'T THAT RIGHT, THOR?
OH, AYE, FRIEND FALCON! A NIGHT OF KEGLING, T'WOULD BE PLEASURABLE INDEED! WHAT SAY THEE, IRON MAN?
OH, I THINK WE MIGHT BE ABLE TO GET IN A GAME OR TWO...!
BOWLING?! HULK LOVES BOWLING!
BUT THESE BALLS TOO PUNY FOR HULK! HULK USE THIS BALL!
TODD DEZAGO WORDS
MARCELO DICHIARA ART
SOTOCOLOR COLOR
DAVE SHARPE LETTERS
MICHAEL HORWITZ ASSISTANT EDITOR
NATHAN COSBY EDITOR
JOE QUESADA EDITOR IN CHIEF
DAN BUCKLEY PUBLISHER
ALAN FINE EXECUTIVE PRODUCER
THE END...

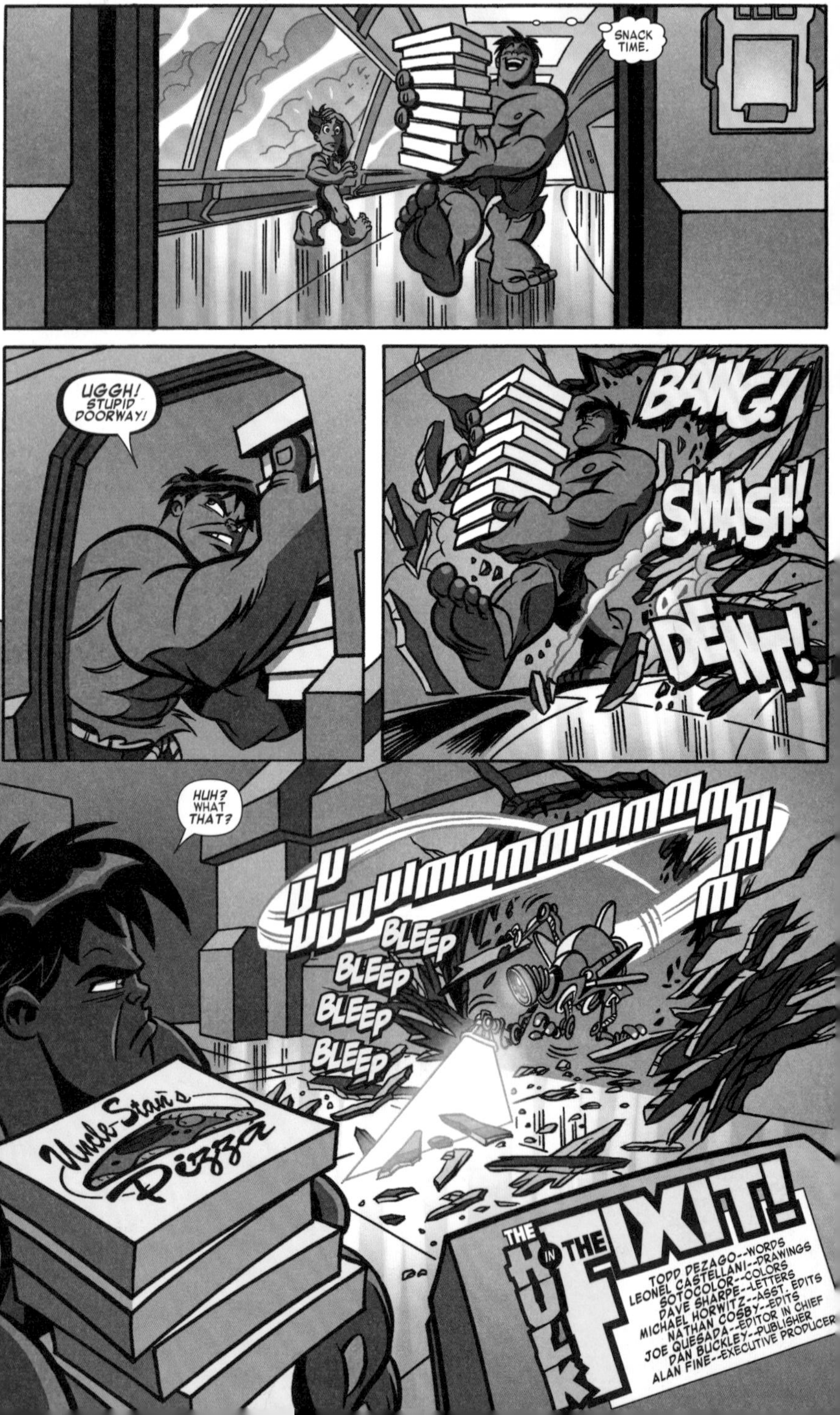
SNACK TIME.
UGGH! STUPID DOORWAY!
BANG!
SMASH!
DENT!
HUH? WHAT THAT?
VVVVVVVMMMMMMMMMMMMMMMMMMM
BLEEP
BLEEP
BLEEP
BLEEP
Uncle Stan's Pizza
THE HULK IN THE FIXIT!
TODD DEZAGO--WORDS
LEONEL CASTELLANI--DRAWINGS
SOTOCOLOR--COLORS
DAVE SHARPE--LETTERS
MICHAEL HORWITZ--ASST. EDITS
NATHAN COSBY--EDITS
JOE QUESADA--EDITOR IN CHIEF
DAN BUCKLEY--PUBLISHER
ALAN FINE--EXECUTIVE PRODUCER

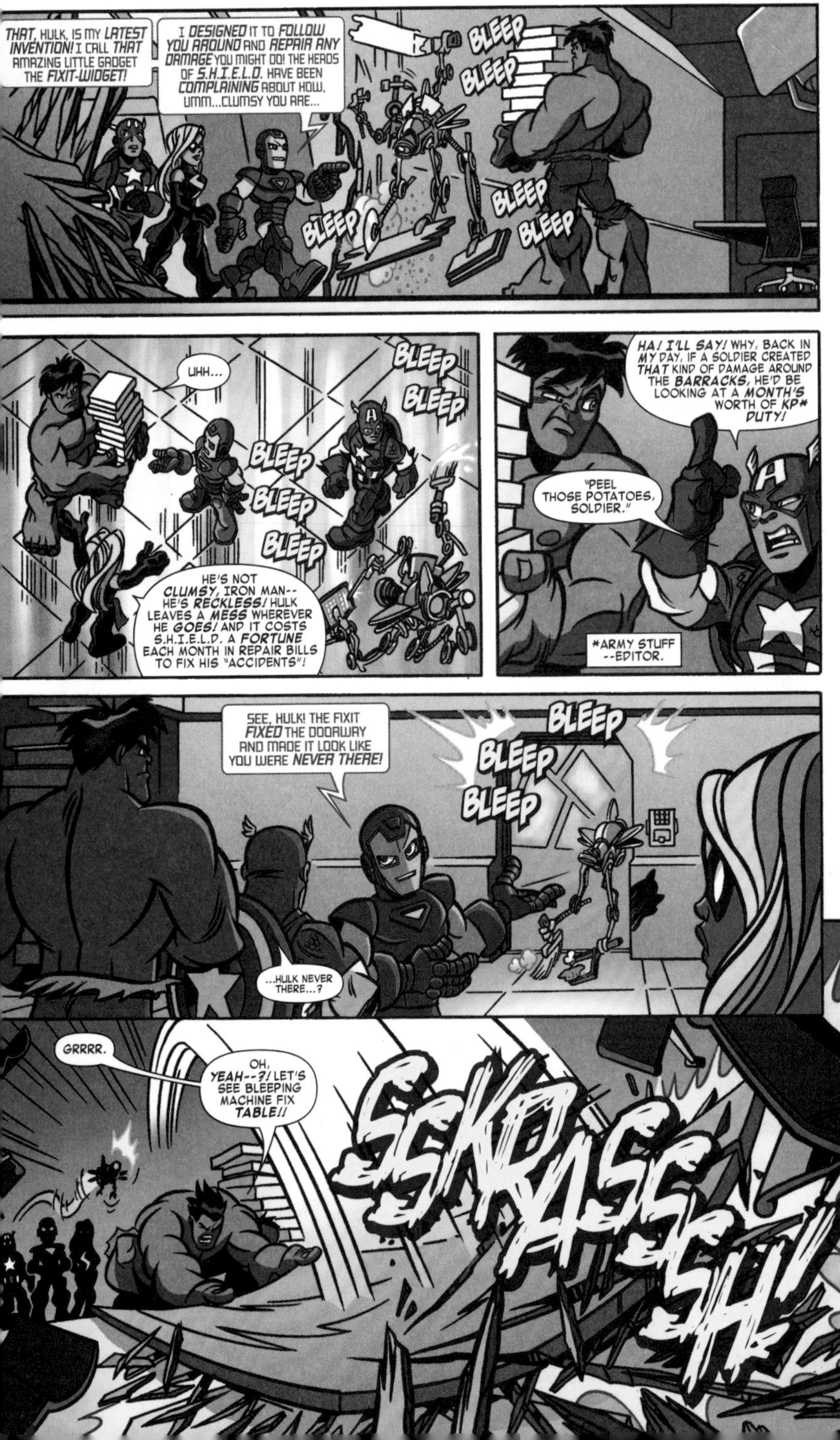
THAT, HULK, IS MY LATEST INVENTION! I CALL THAT AMAZING LITTLE GADGET THE FIXIT-WIDGET!
I DESIGNED IT TO FOLLOW YOU AROUND AND REPAIR ANY DAMAGE YOU MIGHT DO! THE HEROS OF S.H.I.E.L.D. HAVE BEEN COMPLAINING ABOUT HOW, UMM...CLUMSY YOU ARE...
BLEEP
BLEEP
BLEEP
BLEEP
BLEEP
UHH...
BLEEP
BLEEP
BLEEP
BLEEP
BLEEP
HE'S NOT CLUMSY, IRON MAN-- HE'S RECKLESS! HULK LEAVES A MESS WHEREVER HE GOES! AND IT COSTS S.H.I.E.L.D. A FORTUNE EACH MONTH IN REPAIR BILLS TO FIX HIS "ACCIDENTS"!
HA! I'LL SAY! WHY, BACK IN MY DAY, IF A SOLDIER CREATED THAT KIND OF DAMAGE AROUND THE BARRACKS, HE'D BE LOOKING AT A MONTH'S WORTH OF KP* DUTY!
"PEEL THOSE POTATOES, SOLDIER."
*ARMY STUFF --EDITOR.
SEE, HULK! THE FIXIT FIXED THE DOORWAY AND MADE IT LOOK LIKE YOU WERE NEVER THERE!
BLEEP
BLEEP
BLEEP
...HULK NEVER THERE...?
GRRRR.
OH, YEAH--?! LET'S SEE BLEEPING MACHINE FIX TABLE!!
SCKRASSSH!

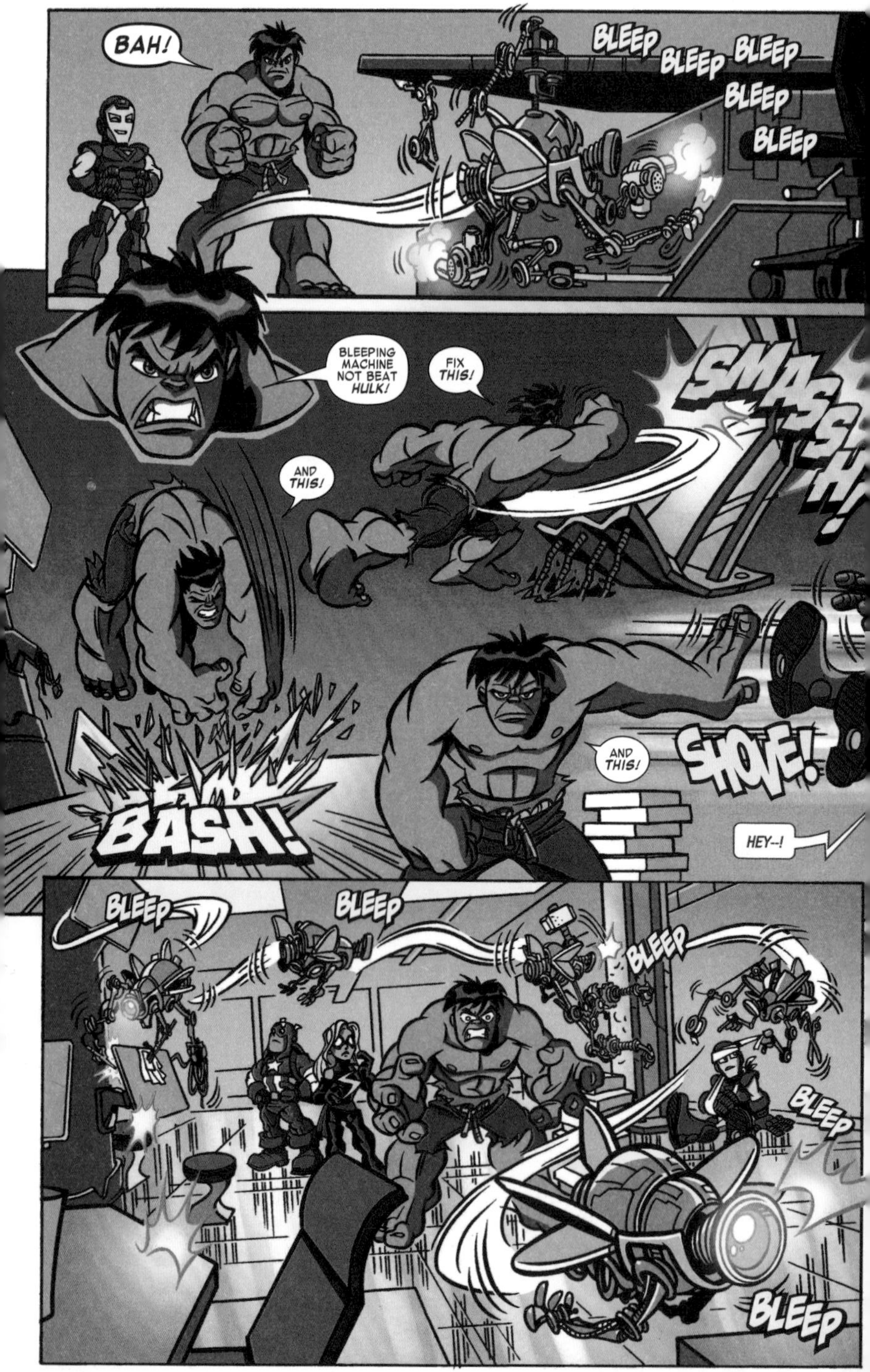
BAH!
BLEEP
BLEEP
BLEEP
BLEEP
BLEEP
BLEEPING MACHINE NOT BEAT HULK!
FIX THIS!
SMASSH!
AND THIS!
BASH!
AND THIS!
SHOVE!
HEY--!
BLEEP
BLEEP
BLEEP
BLEEP
BLEEP

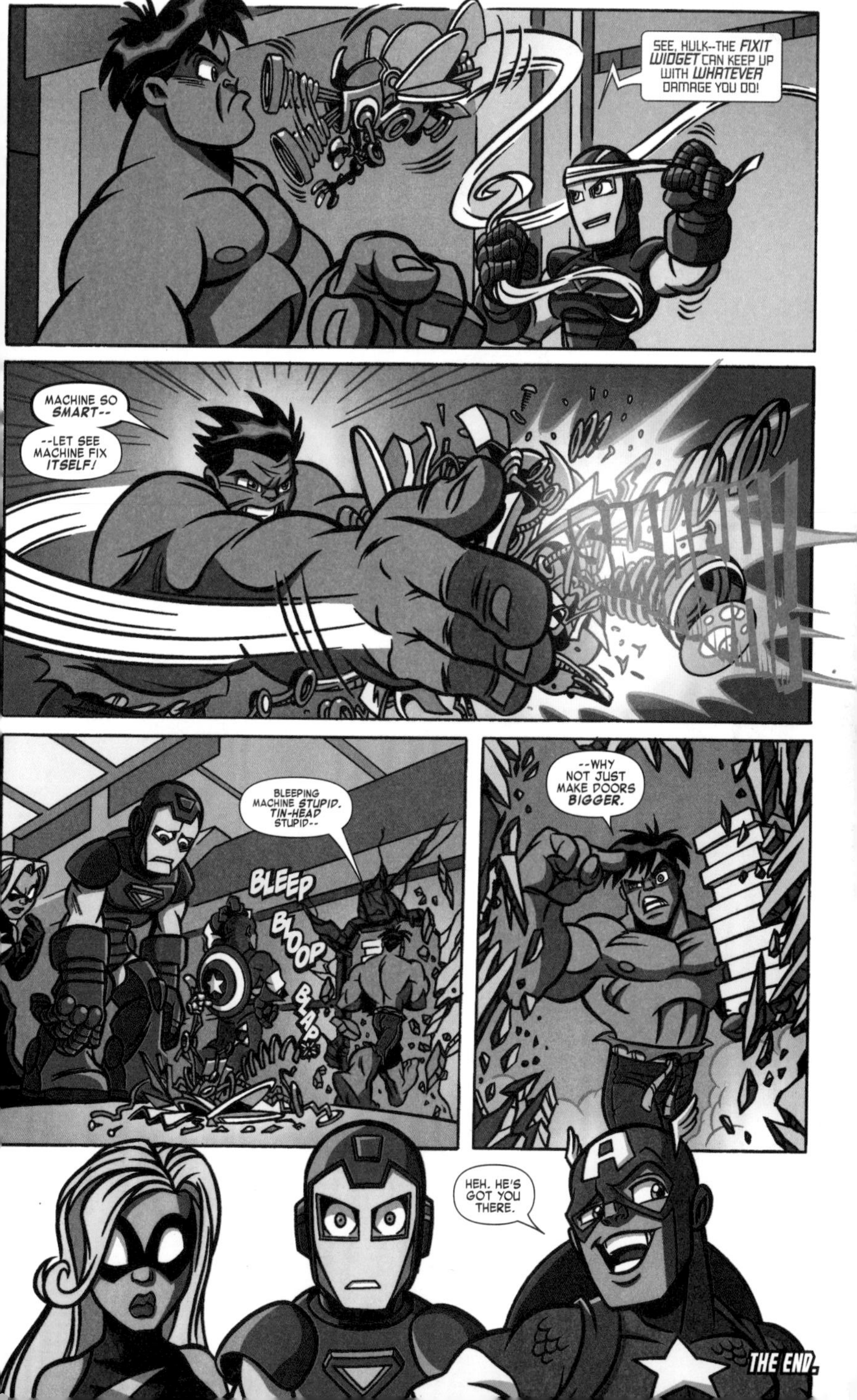
SEE, HULK--THE FIXIT WIDGET CAN KEEP UP WITH WHATEVER DAMAGE YOU DO!
MACHINE SO SMART--
--LET SEE MACHINE FIX ITSELF!
BLEEPING MACHINE STUPID. TIN-HEAD STUPID--
BLEEP
BLOOP
BLAP
--WHY NOT JUST MAKE DOORS BIGGER.
HEH. HE'S GOT YOU THERE.
THE END.

SUPER HERO SQUAD #2

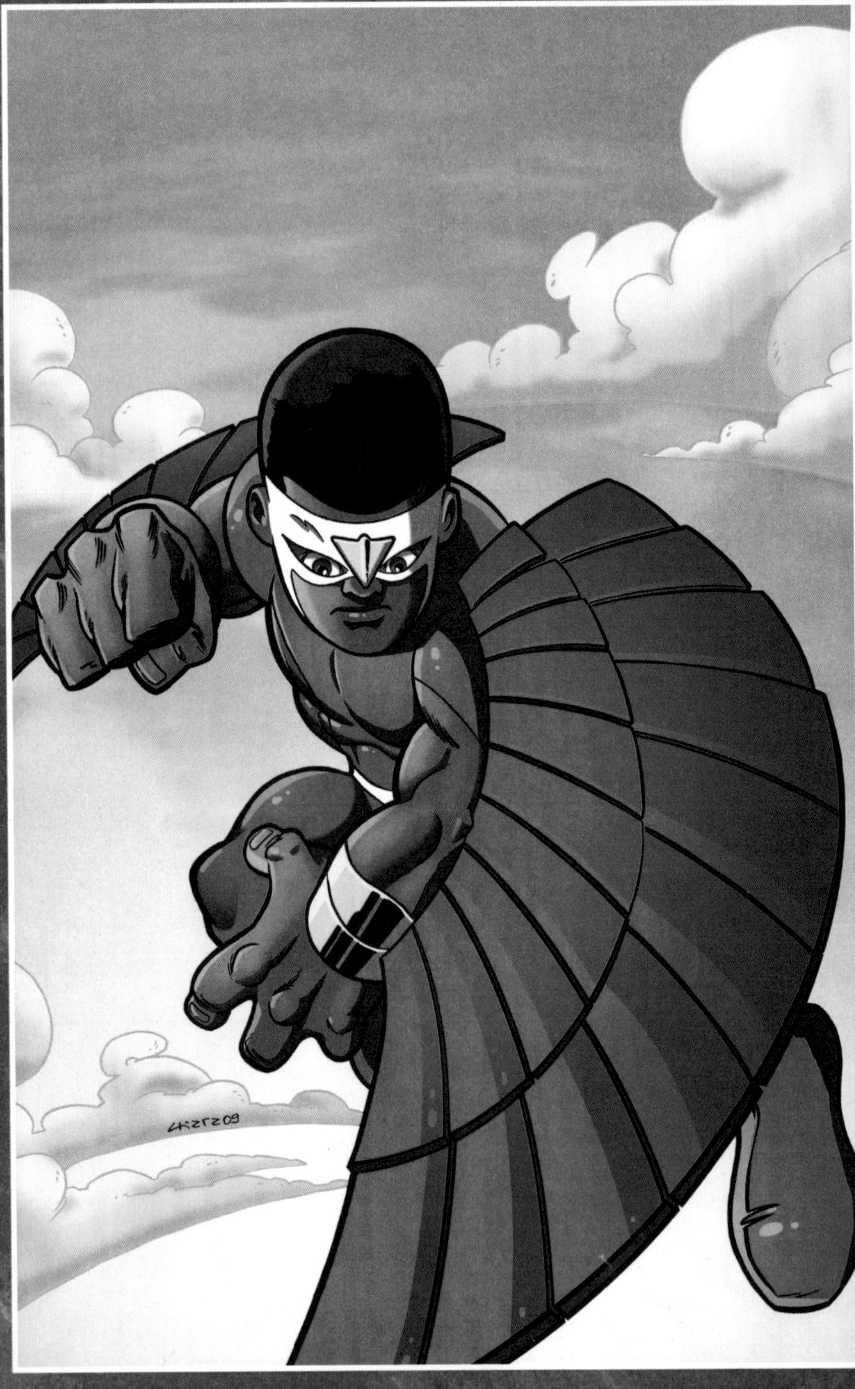

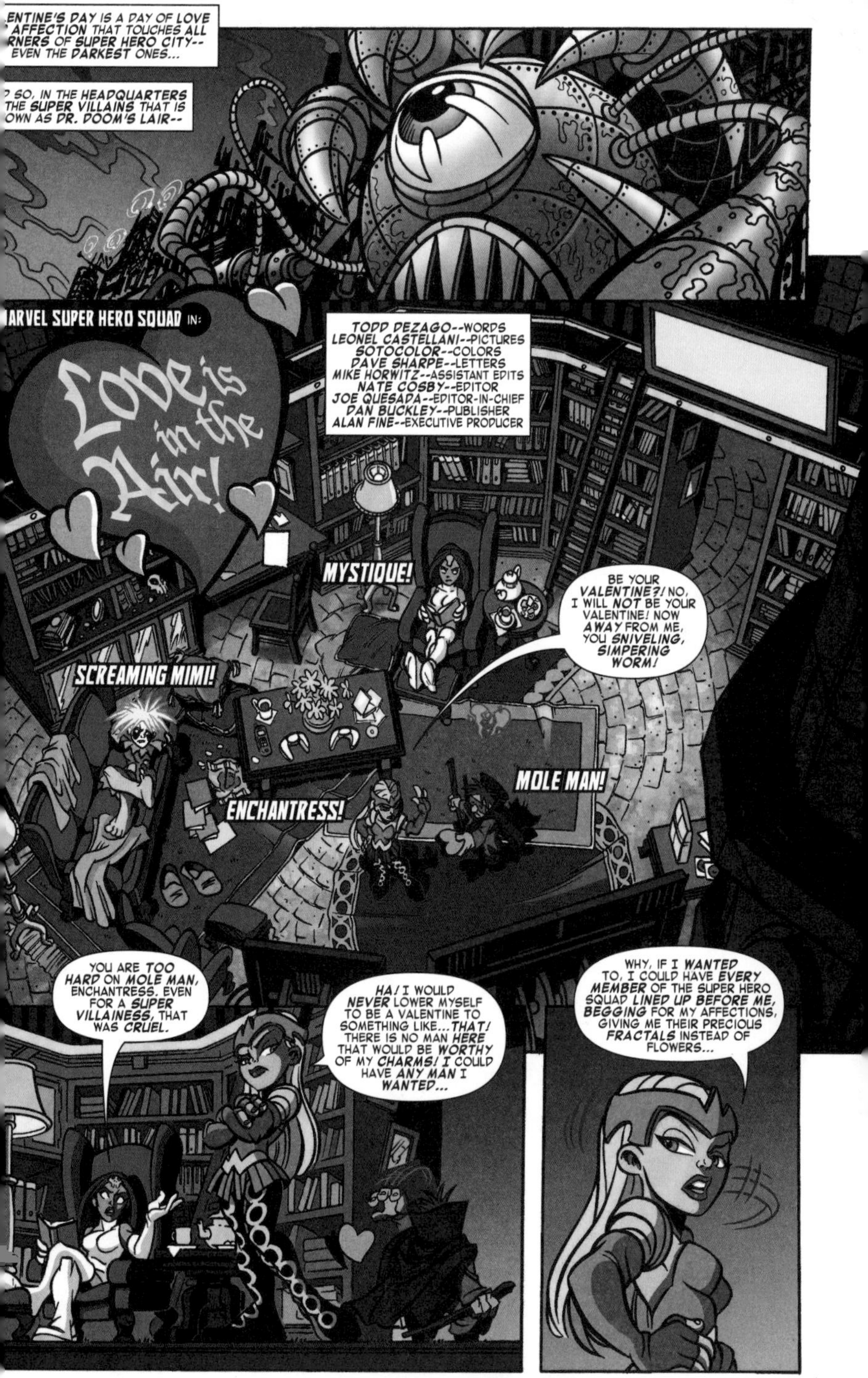

ENTINE'S DAY IS A DAY OF LOVE AFFECTION THAT TOUCHES ALL RNERS OF SUPER HERO CITY-- EVEN THE DARKEST ONES...
SO, IN THE HEADQUARTERS THE SUPER VILLAINS THAT IS OWN AS DR. DOOM'S LAIR--
ARVEL SUPER HERO SQUAD IN:
Love is in the Air!
TODD DEZAGO--WORDS LEONEL CASTELLANI--PICTURES SOTOCOLOR--COLORS DAVE SHARPE--LETTERS MIKE HORWITZ--ASSISTANT EDITS NATE COSBY--EDITOR JOE QUESADA--EDITOR-IN-CHIEF DAN BUCKLEY--PUBLISHER ALAN FINE--EXECUTIVE PRODUCER
MYSTIQUE!
BE YOUR VALENTINE?! NO, I WILL NOT BE YOUR VALENTINE! NOW AWAY FROM ME, YOU SNIVELING, SIMPERING WORM!
SCREAMING MIMI!
MOLE MAN!
ENCHANTRESS!
YOU ARE TOO HARD ON MOLE MAN, ENCHANTRESS. EVEN FOR A SUPER VILLAINESS, THAT WAS CRUEL.
HA! I WOULD NEVER LOWER MYSELF TO BE A VALENTINE TO SOMETHING LIKE...THAT! THERE IS NO MAN HERE THAT WOULD BE WORTHY OF MY CHARMS! I COULD HAVE ANY MAN I WANTED...
WHY, IF I WANTED TO, I COULD HAVE EVERY MEMBER OF THE SUPER HERO SQUAD LINED UP BEFORE ME, BEGGING FOR MY AFFECTIONS, GIVING ME THEIR PRECIOUS FRACTALS INSTEAD OF FLOWERS...

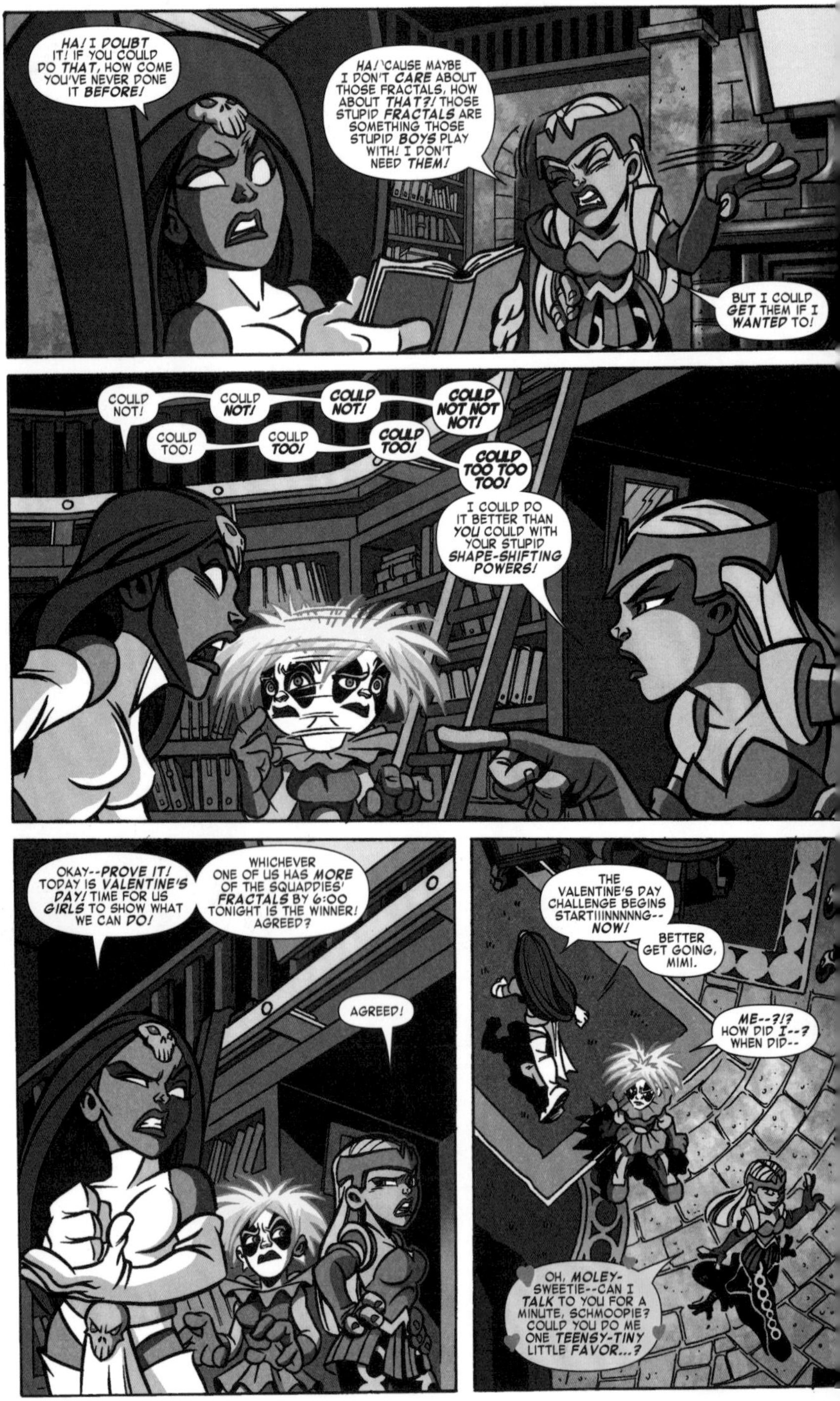
HA! I DOUBT IT! IF YOU COULD DO THAT, HOW COME YOU'VE NEVER DONE IT BEFORE!
HA! 'CAUSE MAYBE I DON'T CARE ABOUT THOSE FRACTALS, HOW ABOUT THAT?! THOSE STUPID FRACTALS ARE SOMETHING THOSE STUPID BOYS PLAY WITH! I DON'T NEED THEM!
BUT I COULD GET THEM IF I WANTED TO!
COULD NOT!
COULD TOO!
COULD NOT!
COULD TOO!
COULD NOT!
COULD TOO!
COULD NOT NOT NOT!
COULD TOO TOO TOO!
I COULD DO IT BETTER THAN YOU COULD WITH YOUR STUPID SHAPE-SHIFTING POWERS!
OKAY--PROVE IT! TODAY IS VALENTINE'S DAY! TIME FOR US GIRLS TO SHOW WHAT WE CAN DO!
WHICHEVER ONE OF US HAS MORE OF THE SQUADDIES' FRACTALS BY 6:00 TONIGHT IS THE WINNER! AGREED?
AGREED!
THE VALENTINE'S DAY CHALLENGE BEGINS STARTIIIINNNNNG--NOW!
BETTER GET GOING, MIMI.
ME--?!? HOW DID I--? WHEN DID--
OH, MOLEY-SWEETIE--CAN I TALK TO YOU FOR A MINUTE, SCHMOOPIE? COULD YOU DO ME ONE TEENSY-TINY LITTLE FAVOR...?

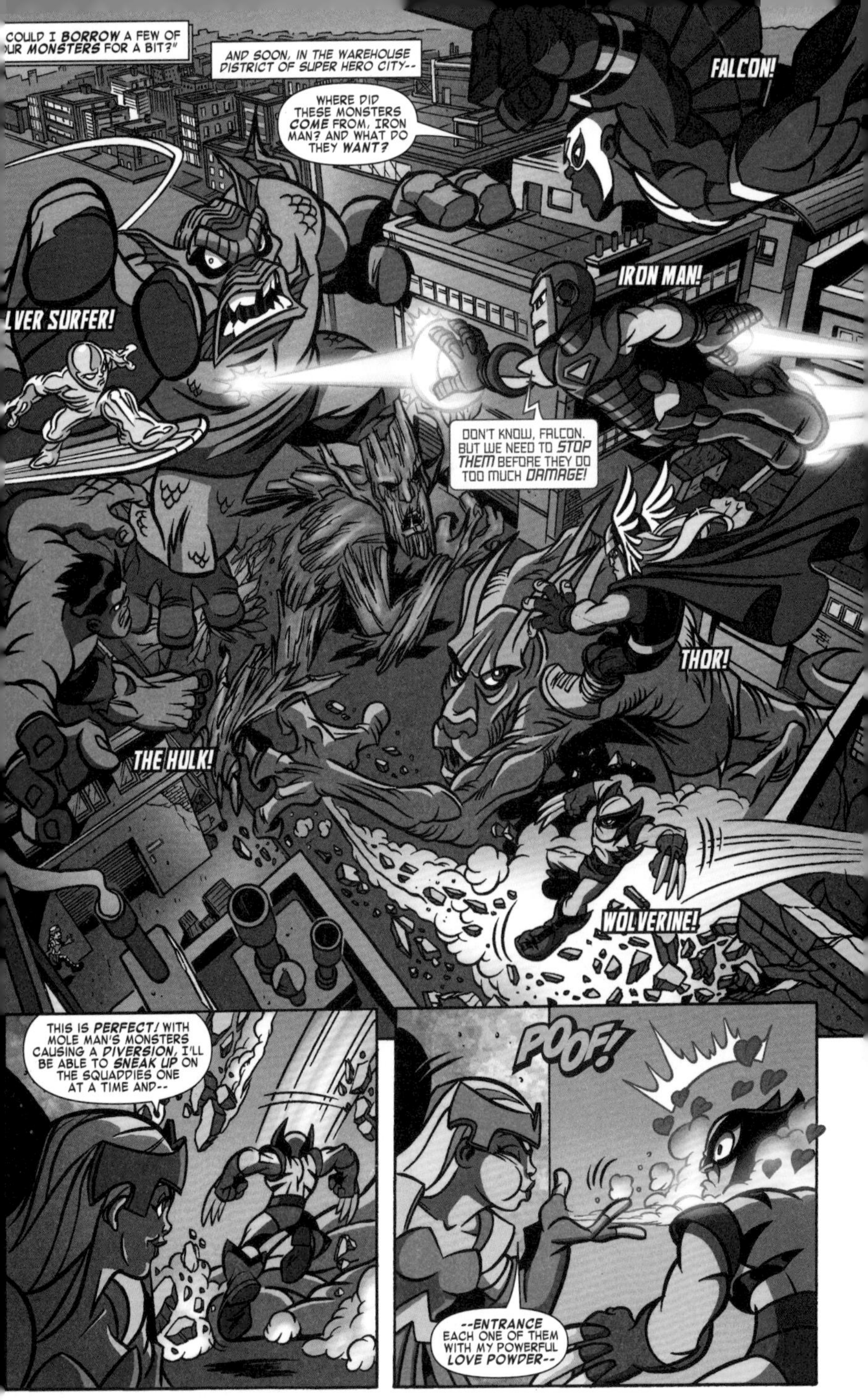

COULD I BORROW A FEW OF
UR MONSTERS FOR A BIT?"
AND SOON, IN THE WAREHOUSE DISTRICT OF SUPER HERO CITY--
FALCON!
WHERE DID THESE MONSTERS COME FROM, IRON MAN? AND WHAT DO THEY WANT?
IRON MAN!
LVER SURFER!
DON'T KNOW, FALCON. BUT WE NEED TO STOP THEM BEFORE THEY DO TOO MUCH DAMAGE!
THOR!
THE HULK!
WOLVERINE!
THIS IS PERFECT! WITH MOLE MAN'S MONSTERS CAUSING A DIVERSION, I'LL BE ABLE TO SNEAK UP ON THE SQUADDIES ONE AT A TIME AND--
POOF!
--ENTRANCE EACH ONE OF THEM WITH MY POWERFUL LOVE POWDER--

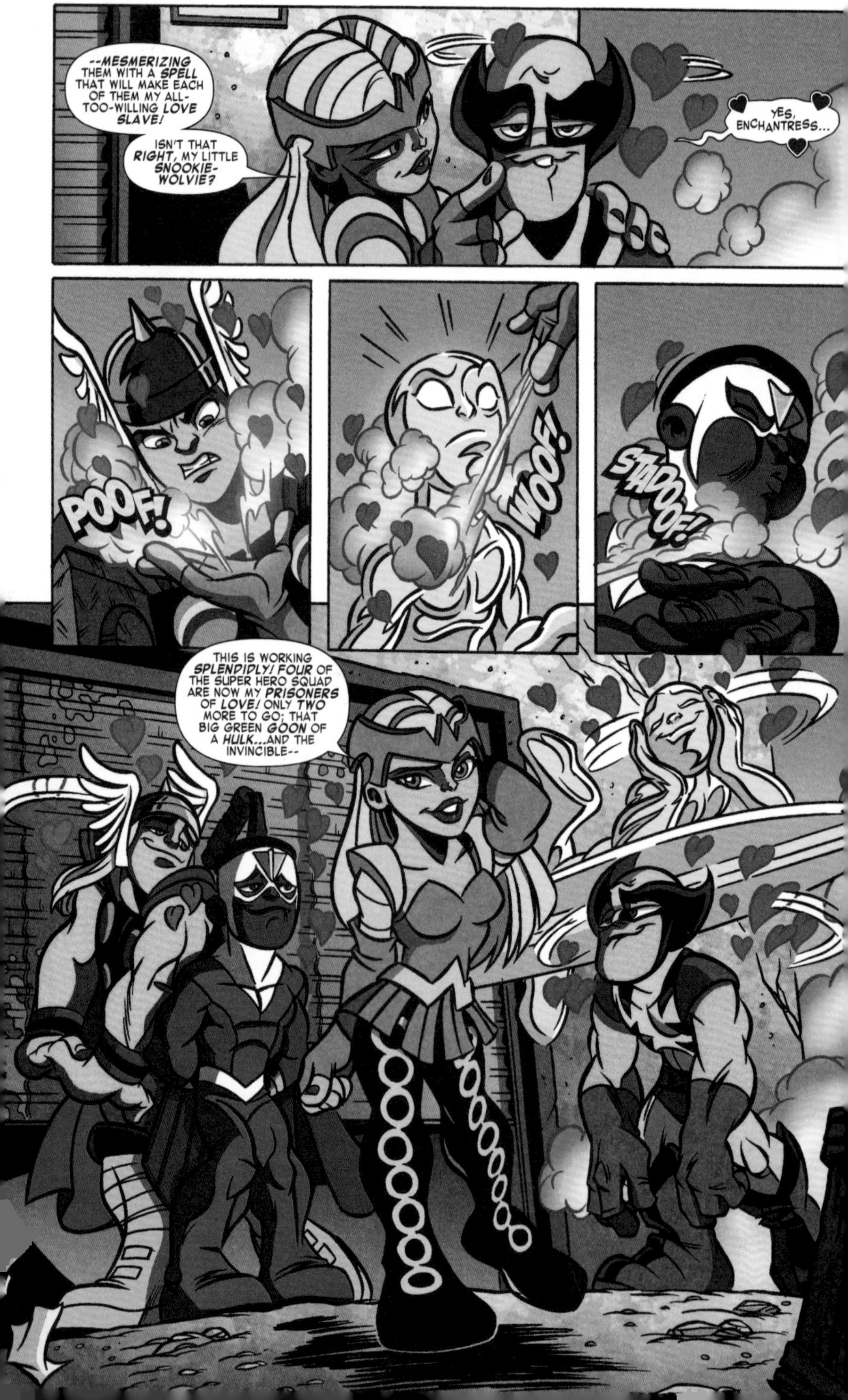
--MESMERIZING THEM WITH A SPELL THAT WILL MAKE EACH OF THEM MY ALL-TOO-WILLING LOVE SLAVE!
ISN'T THAT RIGHT, MY LITTLE SNOOKIE-WOLVIE?
YES, ENCHANTRESS...
POOF!
WOOF!
STADOOF!
THIS IS WORKING SPLENDIDLY! FOUR OF THE SUPER HERO SQUAD ARE NOW MY PRISONERS OF LOVE! ONLY TWO MORE TO GO; THAT BIG GREEN GOON OF A HULK...AND THE INVINCIBLE--

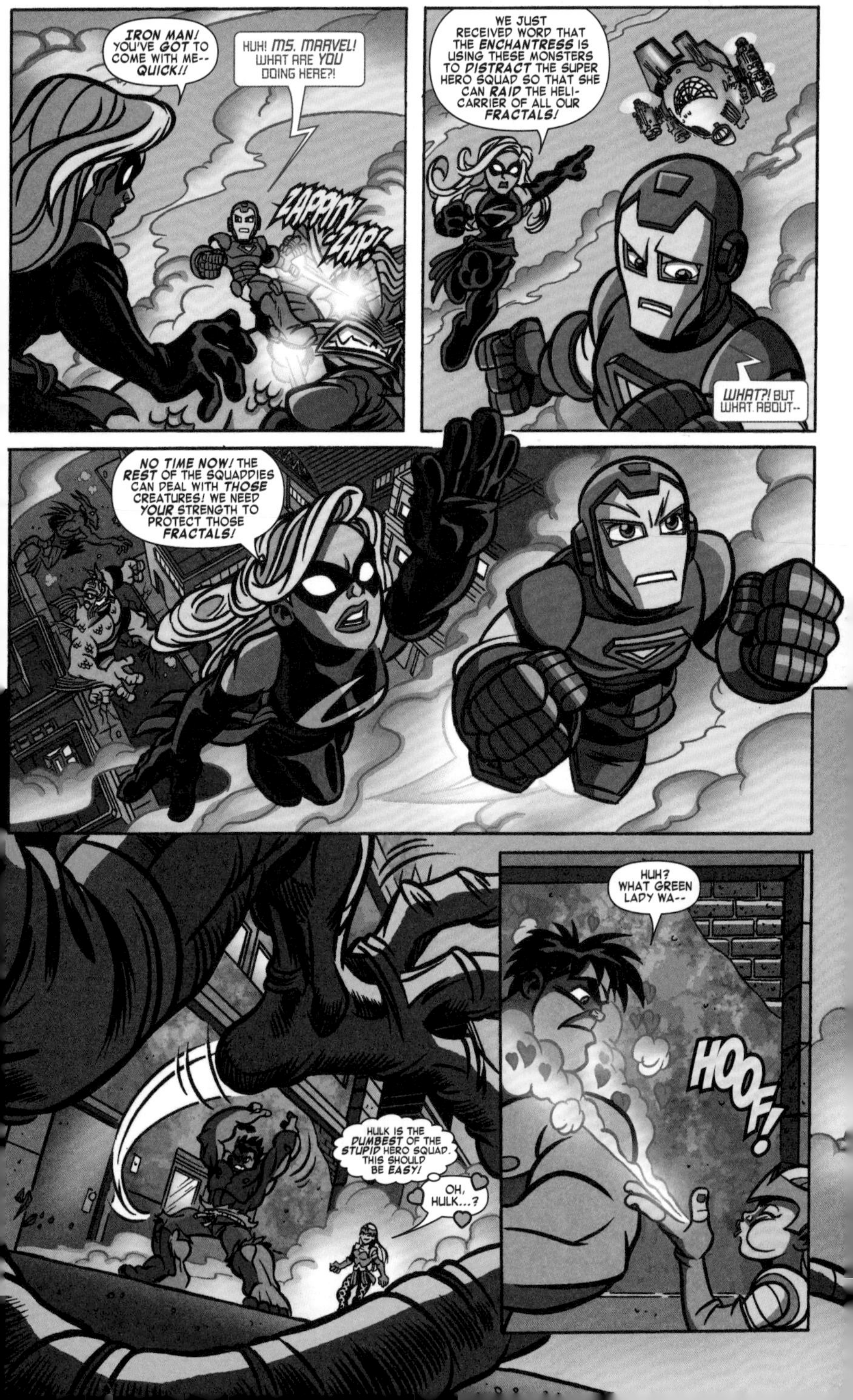
IRON MAN! YOU'VE GOT TO COME WITH ME-- QUICK!!
HUH! MS. MARVEL! WHAT ARE YOU DOING HERE?!
ZAPPITY ZAP!
WE JUST RECEIVED WORD THAT THE ENCHANTRESS IS USING THESE MONSTERS TO DISTRACT THE SUPER HERO SQUAD SO THAT SHE CAN RAID THE HELI-CARRIER OF ALL OUR FRACTALS!
WHAT?! BUT WHAT ABOUT--
NO TIME NOW! THE REST OF THE SQUADDIES CAN DEAL WITH THOSE CREATURES! WE NEED YOUR STRENGTH TO PROTECT THOSE FRACTALS!
HULK IS THE DUMBEST OF THE STUPID HERO SQUAD. THIS SHOULD BE EASY!
OH, HULK...?
HUH? WHAT GREEN LADY WA--
HOOF!

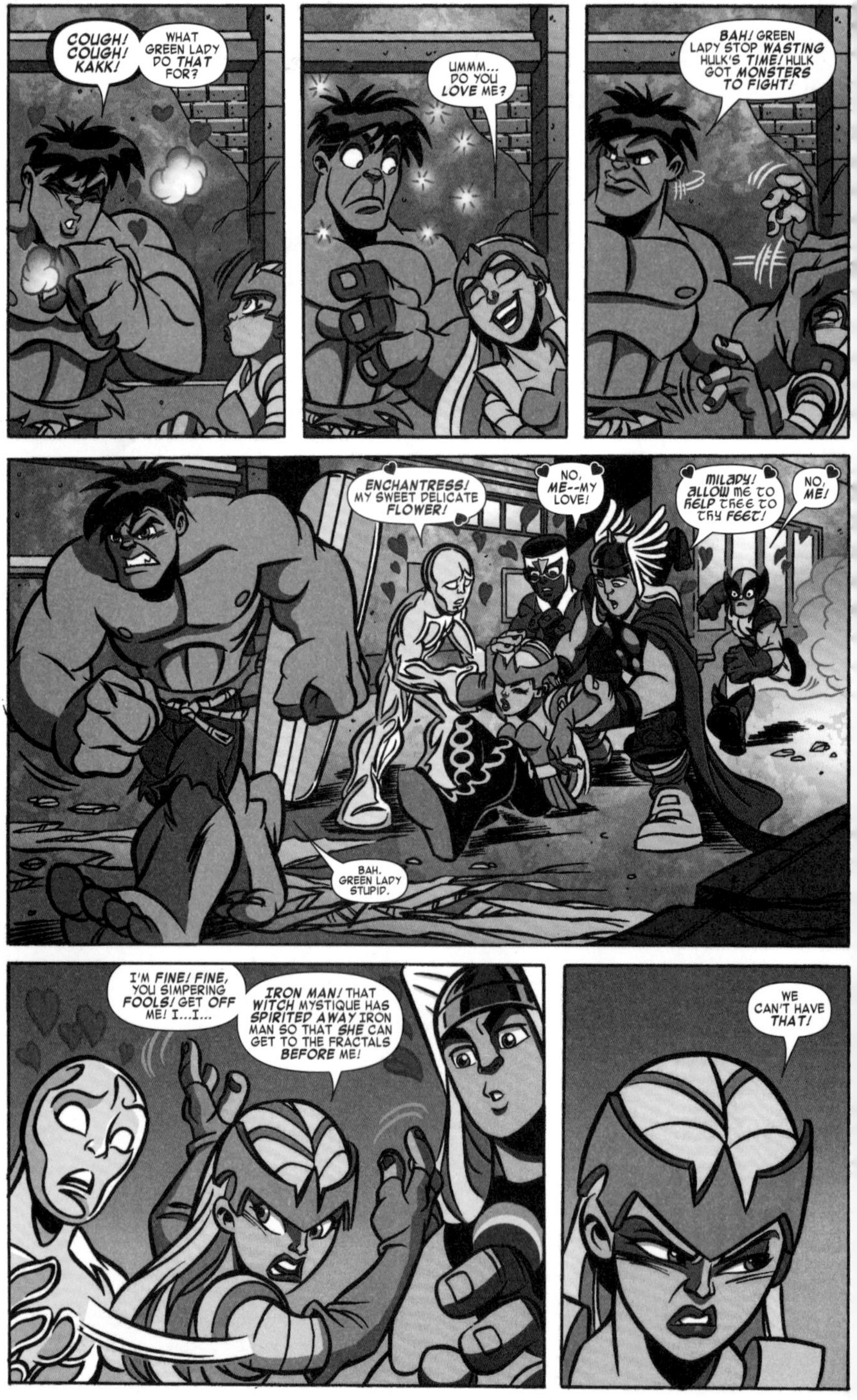
COUGH! COUGH! KAKK!
WHAT GREEN LADY DO THAT FOR?
UMMM... DO YOU LOVE ME?
BAH! GREEN LADY STOP WASTING HULK'S TIME! HULK GOT MONSTERS TO FIGHT!
ENCHANTRESS! MY SWEET DELICATE FLOWER!
NO, ME--MY LOVE!
MILADY! ALLOW ME TO HELP THEE TO THY FEET!
NO, ME!
BAH. GREEN LADY STUPID.
I'M FINE! FINE, YOU SIMPERING FOOLS! GET OFF ME! I...I...
IRON MAN! THAT WITCH MYSTIQUE HAS SPIRITED AWAY IRON MAN SO THAT SHE CAN GET TO THE FRACTALS BEFORE ME!
WE CAN'T HAVE THAT!

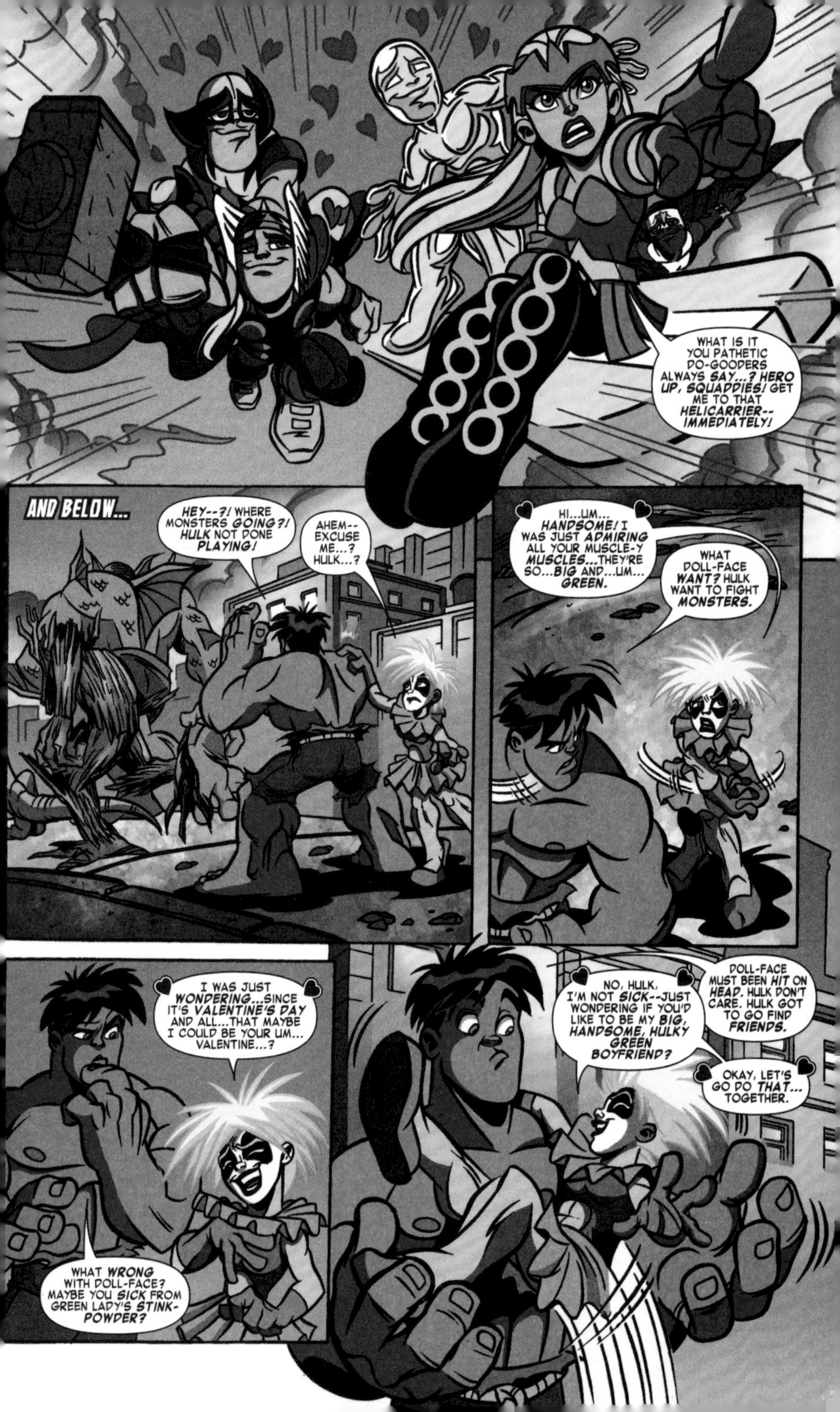

WHAT IS IT YOU PATHETIC DO-GOODERS ALWAYS SAY...? HERO UP, SQUADDIES! GET ME TO THAT HELICARRIER-- IMMEDIATELY!
AND BELOW...
HEY--?! WHERE MONSTERS GOING?! HULK NOT DONE PLAYING!
AHEM-- EXCUSE ME...? HULK...?
HI...UM... HANDSOME! I WAS JUST ADMIRING ALL YOUR MUSCLE-Y MUSCLES...THEY'RE SO...BIG AND...UM... GREEN.
WHAT DOLL-FACE WANT? HULK WANT TO FIGHT MONSTERS.
I WAS JUST WONDERING...SINCE IT'S VALENTINE'S DAY AND ALL...THAT MAYBE I COULD BE YOUR UM... VALENTINE...?
WHAT WRONG WITH DOLL-FACE? MAYBE YOU SICK FROM GREEN LADY'S STINK-POWDER?
NO, HULK, I'M NOT SICK--JUST WONDERING IF YOU'D LIKE TO BE MY BIG, HANDSOME, HULKY GREEN BOYFRIEND?
DOLL-FACE MUST BEEN HIT ON HEAD. HULK DON'T CARE. HULK GOT TO GO FIND FRIENDS.
OKAY, LET'S GO DO THAT... TOGETHER.

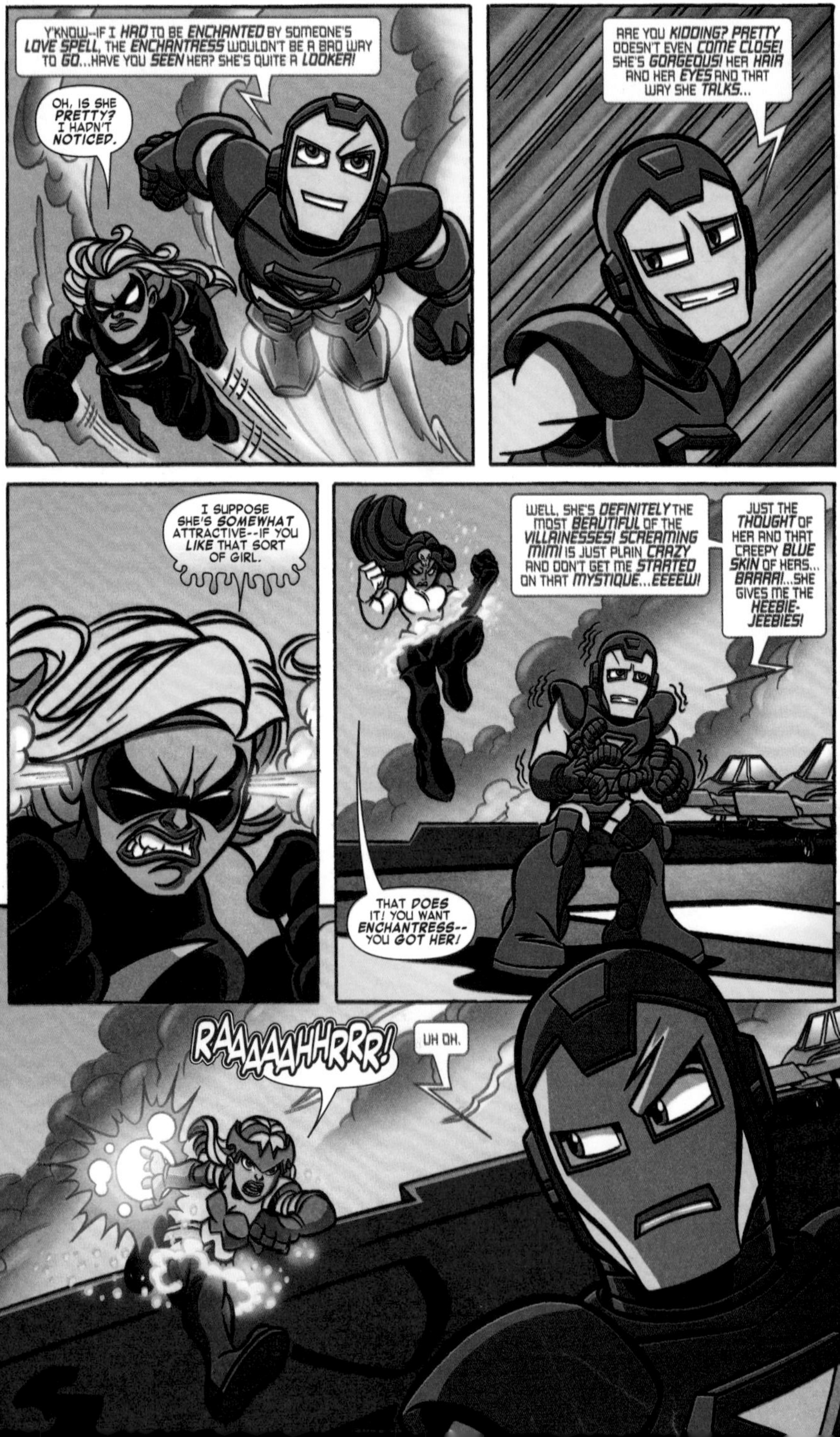
Y'KNOW--IF I HAD TO BE ENCHANTED BY SOMEONE'S LOVE SPELL, THE ENCHANTRESS WOULDN'T BE A BAD WAY TO GO...HAVE YOU SEEN HER? SHE'S QUITE A LOOKER!
OH, IS SHE PRETTY? I HADN'T NOTICED.
ARE YOU KIDDING? PRETTY DOESN'T EVEN COME CLOSE! SHE'S GORGEOUS! HER HAIR AND HER EYES AND THAT WAY SHE TALKS...
I SUPPOSE SHE'S SOMEWHAT ATTRACTIVE--IF YOU LIKE THAT SORT OF GIRL.
WELL, SHE'S DEFINITELY THE MOST BEAUTIFUL OF THE VILLAINESSES! SCREAMING MIMI IS JUST PLAIN CRAZY AND DON'T GET ME STARTED ON THAT MYSTIQUE...EEEEW!
JUST THE THOUGHT OF HER AND THAT CREEPY BLUE SKIN OF HERS... BRRRR!...SHE GIVES ME THE HEEBIE-JEEBIES!
THAT DOES IT! YOU WANT ENCHANTRESS--YOU GOT HER!
RAAAAAHHRRR!
UH OH.

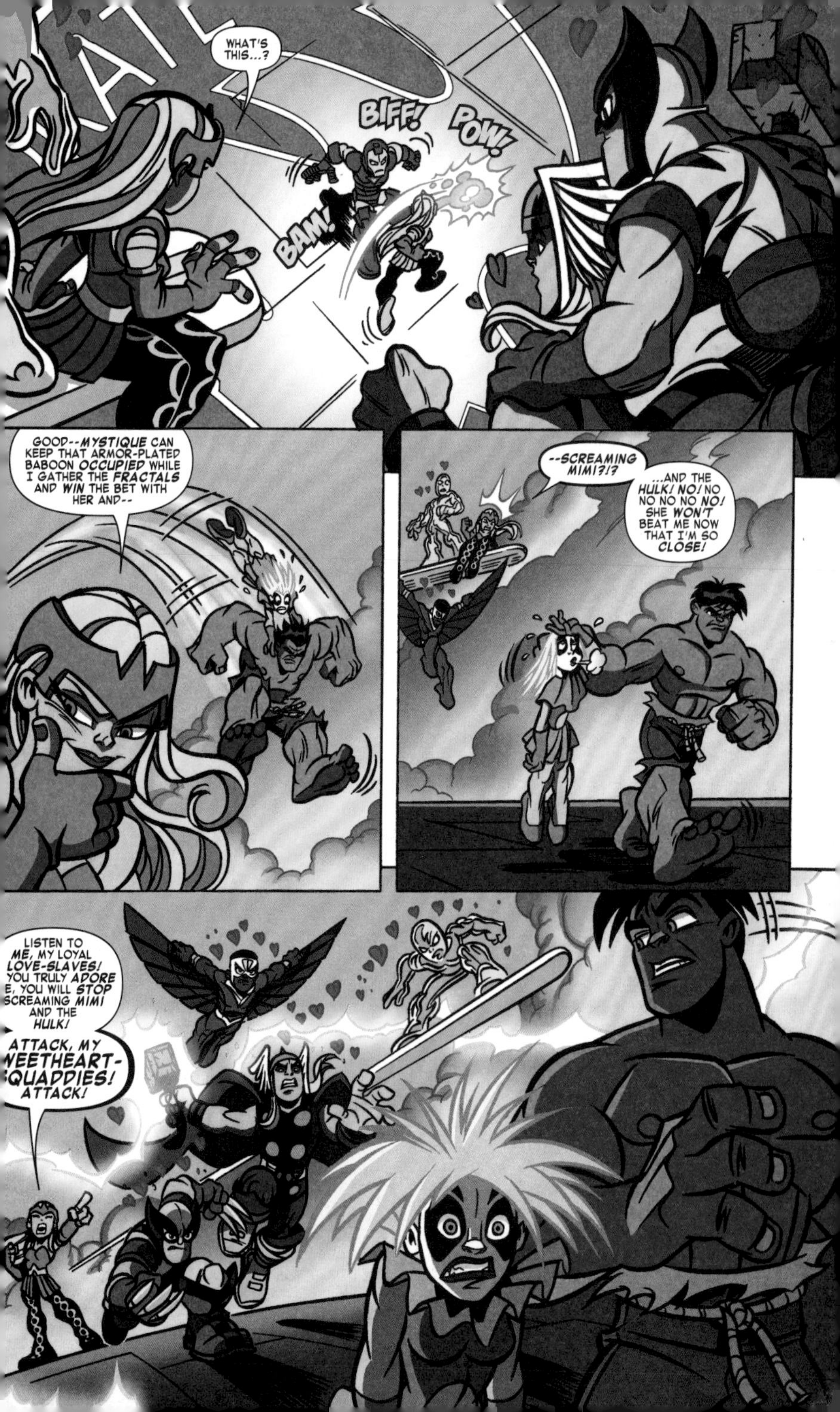
WHAT'S THIS...?
BIFF!
POW!
BAM!
GOOD--MYSTIQUE CAN KEEP THAT ARMOR-PLATED BABOON OCCUPIED WHILE I GATHER THE FRACTALS AND WIN THE BET WITH HER AND--
--SCREAMING MIMI?!?
...AND THE HULK! NO! NO NO NO NO NO! SHE WON'T BEAT ME NOW THAT I'M SO CLOSE!
LISTEN TO ME, MY LOYAL LOVE-SLAVES! YOU TRULY ADORE E, YOU WILL STOP SCREAMING MIMI AND THE HULK!
ATTACK, MY WEETHEART-QUADDIES! ATTACK!

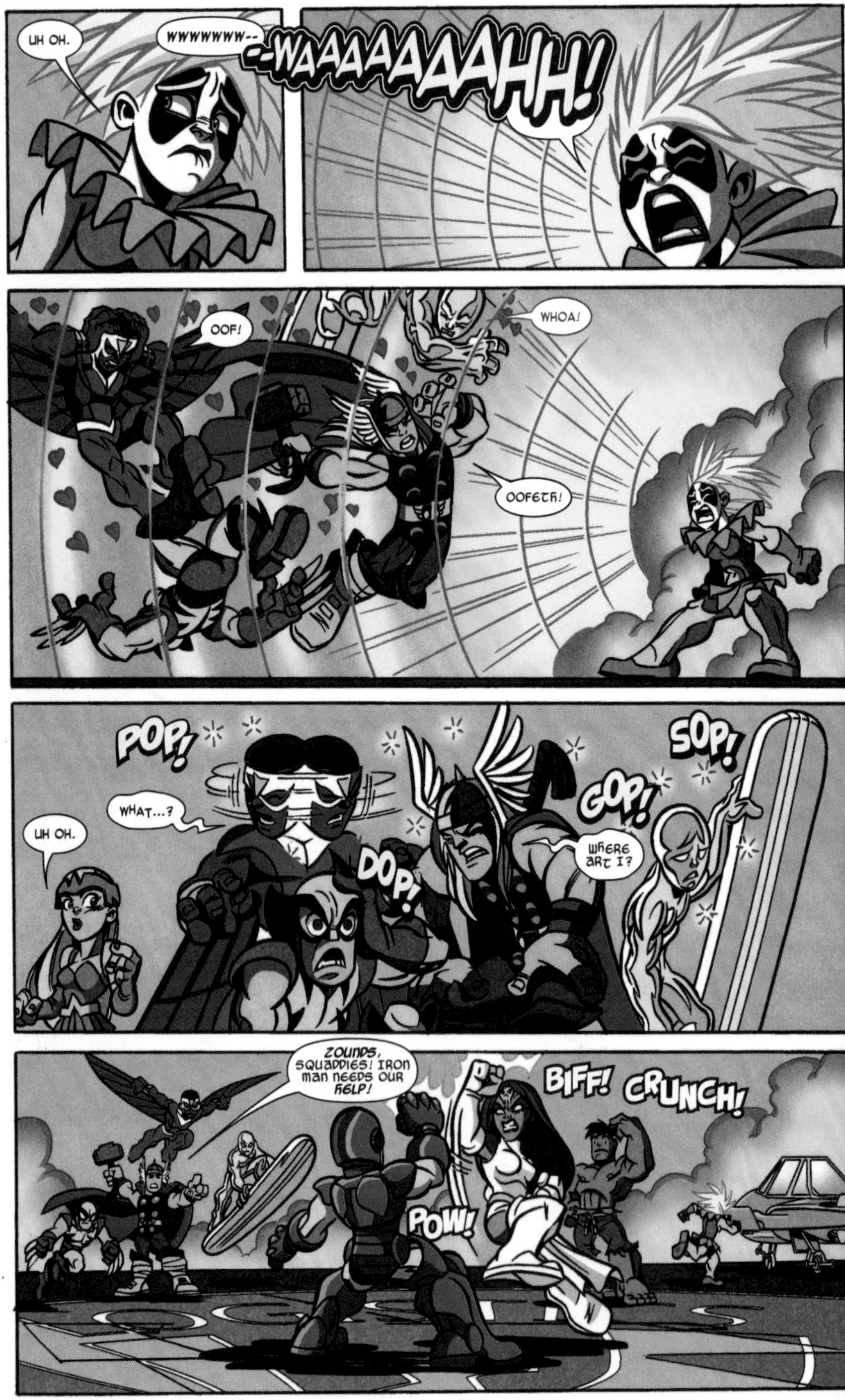
UH OH.
WWWWWWW--
--WAAAAAAAHH!
OOF!
WHOA!
OOFETH!
POP!
WHAT...?
UH OH.
DOP!
GOP!
SOP!
WHERE ART I?
ZOUNDS, SQUADDIES! IRON MAN NEEDS OUR HELP!
BIFF! CRUNCH!
POW!

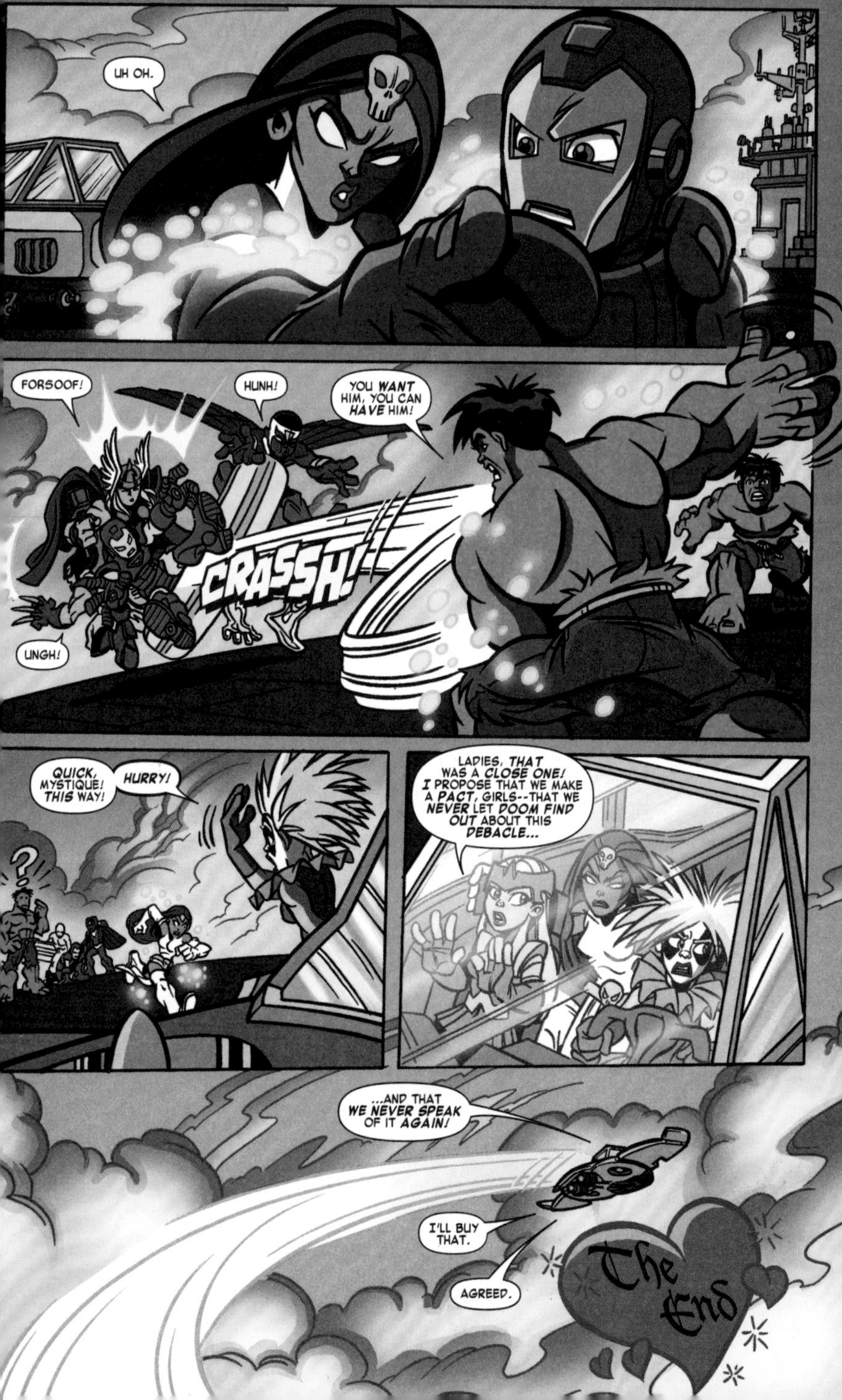
UH OH.
FORSOOF!
HUNH!
YOU WANT HIM, YOU CAN HAVE HIM!
CRASSH!
UNGH!
QUICK, MYSTIQUE! THIS WAY!
HURRY!
?
LADIES, THAT WAS A CLOSE ONE! I PROPOSE THAT WE MAKE A PACT, GIRLS--THAT WE NEVER LET DOOM FIND OUT ABOUT THIS DEBACLE...
...AND THAT WE NEVER SPEAK OF IT AGAIN!
I'LL BUY THAT.
AGREED.
The End

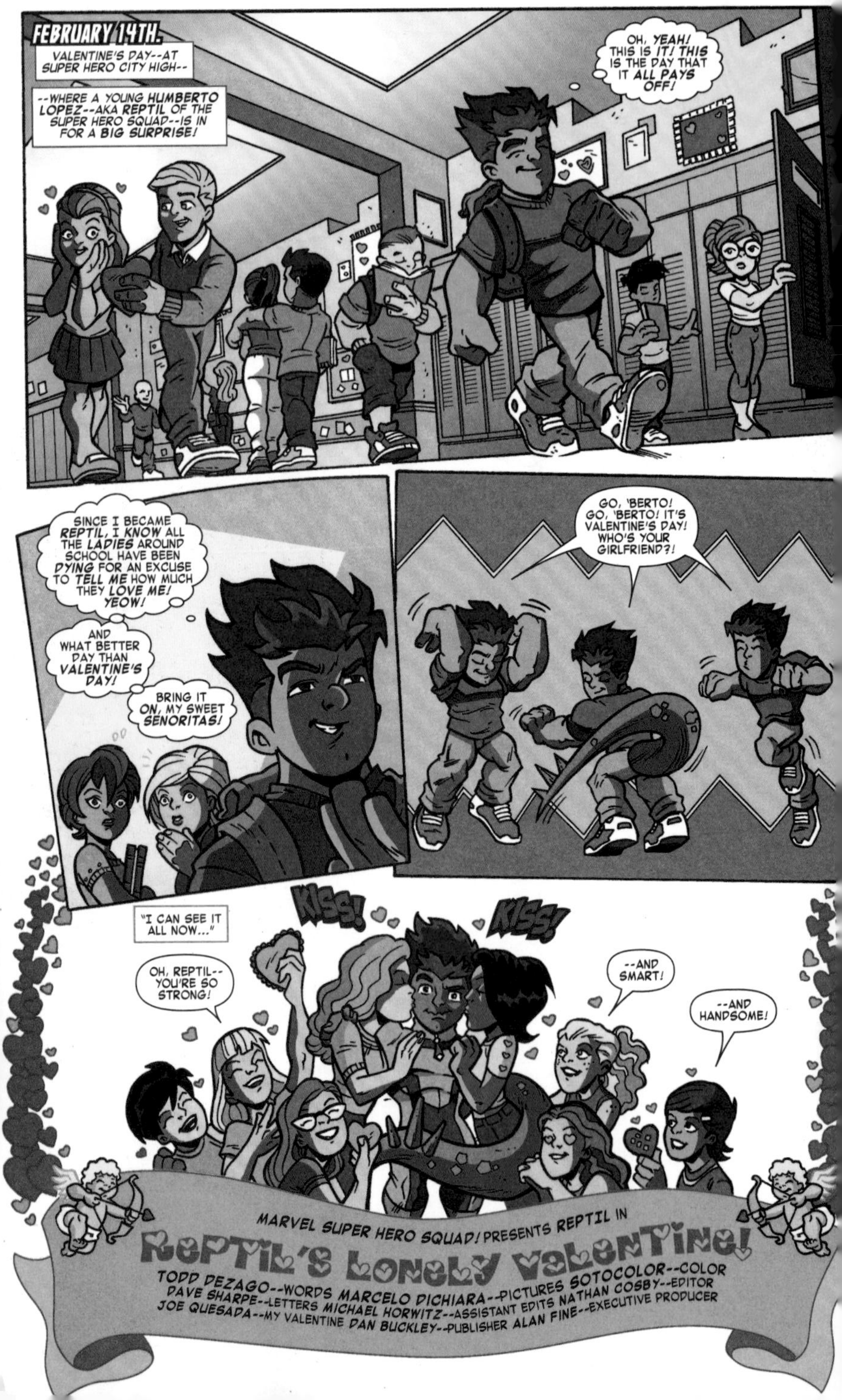
FEBRUARY 14TH.
VALENTINE'S DAY--AT SUPER HERO CITY HIGH--
--WHERE A YOUNG HUMBERTO LOPEZ--AKA REPTIL OF THE SUPER HERO SQUAD--IS IN FOR A BIG SURPRISE!
OH, YEAH! THIS IS IT! THIS IS THE DAY THAT IT ALL PAYS OFF!
SINCE I BECAME REPTIL, I KNOW ALL THE LADIES AROUND SCHOOL HAVE BEEN DYING FOR AN EXCUSE TO TELL ME HOW MUCH THEY LOVE ME! YEOW!
AND WHAT BETTER DAY THAN VALENTINE'S DAY!
BRING IT ON, MY SWEET SEÑORITAS!
GO, 'BERTO! GO, 'BERTO! IT'S VALENTINE'S DAY! WHO'S YOUR GIRLFRIEND?!
"I CAN SEE IT ALL NOW..."
KISS!
KISS!
OH, REPTIL-- YOU'RE SO STRONG!
--AND SMART!
--AND HANDSOME!
MARVEL SUPER HERO SQUAD! PRESENTS REPTIL IN
REPTIL'S LONELY VALENTINE!
TODD DEZAGO--WORDS MARCELO DICHIARA--PICTURES SOTOCOLOR--COLOR
DAVE SHARPE--LETTERS MICHAEL HORWITZ--ASSISTANT EDITS NATHAN COSBY--EDITOR
JOE QUESADA--MY VALENTINE DAN BUCKLEY--PUBLISHER ALAN FINE--EXECUTIVE PRODUCER

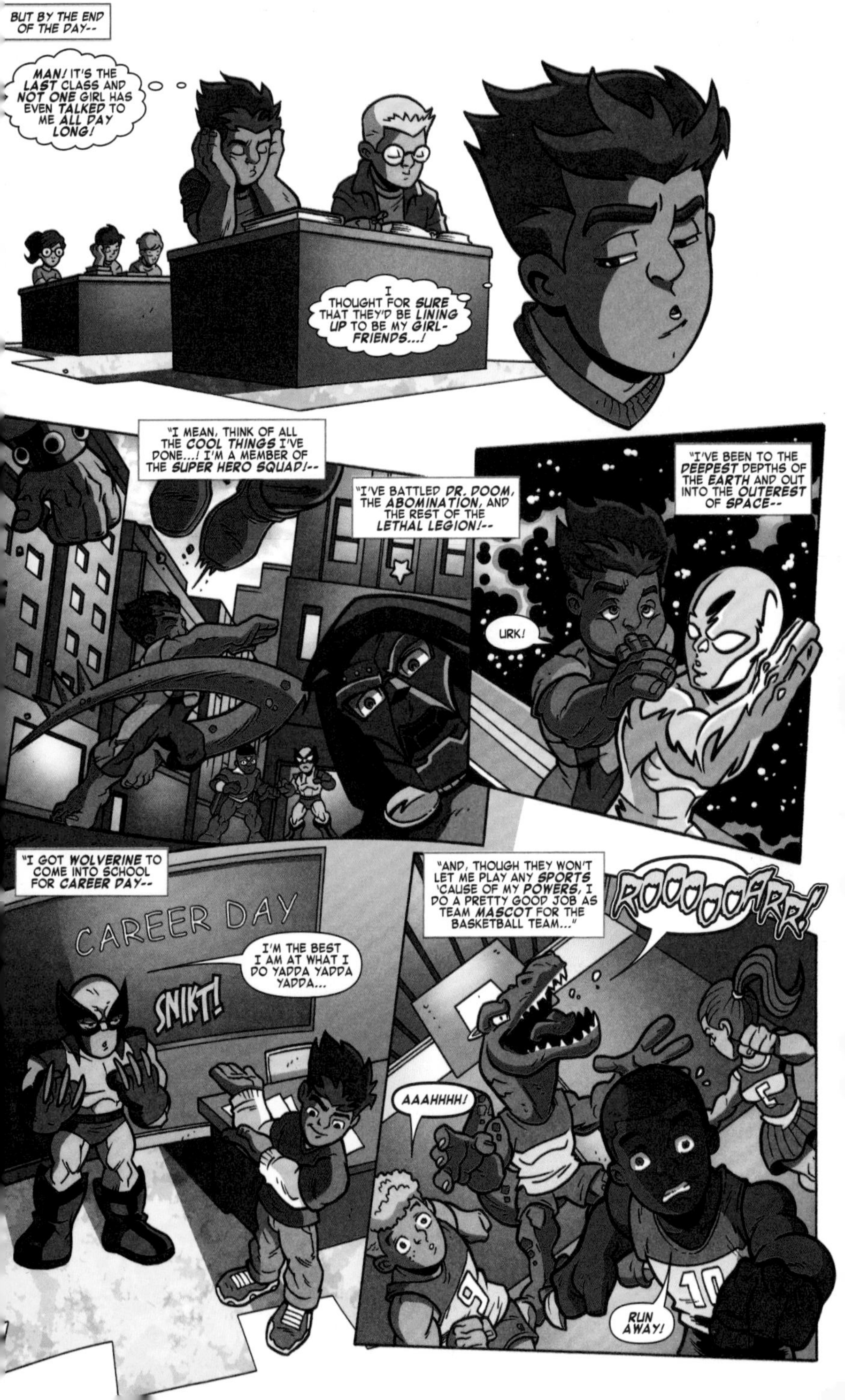
BUT BY THE END OF THE DAY--
MAN! IT'S THE LAST CLASS AND NOT ONE GIRL HAS EVEN TALKED TO ME ALL DAY LONG!
I THOUGHT FOR SURE THAT THEY'D BE LINING UP TO BE MY GIRL-FRIENDS...!
"I MEAN, THINK OF ALL THE COOL THINGS I'VE DONE...! I'M A MEMBER OF THE SUPER HERO SQUAD!--
"I'VE BATTLED DR. DOOM, THE ABOMINATION, AND THE REST OF THE LETHAL LEGION!--
"I'VE BEEN TO THE DEEPEST DEPTHS OF THE EARTH AND OUT INTO THE OUTEREST OF SPACE--
URK!
"I GOT WOLVERINE TO COME INTO SCHOOL FOR CAREER DAY--
CAREER DAY
I'M THE BEST I AM AT WHAT I DO YADDA YADDA YADDA...
SNIKT!
"AND, THOUGH THEY WON'T LET ME PLAY ANY SPORTS 'CAUSE OF MY POWERS, I DO A PRETTY GOOD JOB AS TEAM MASCOT FOR THE BASKETBALL TEAM..."
ROOOOOARR!
AAAHHHH!
RUN AWAY!

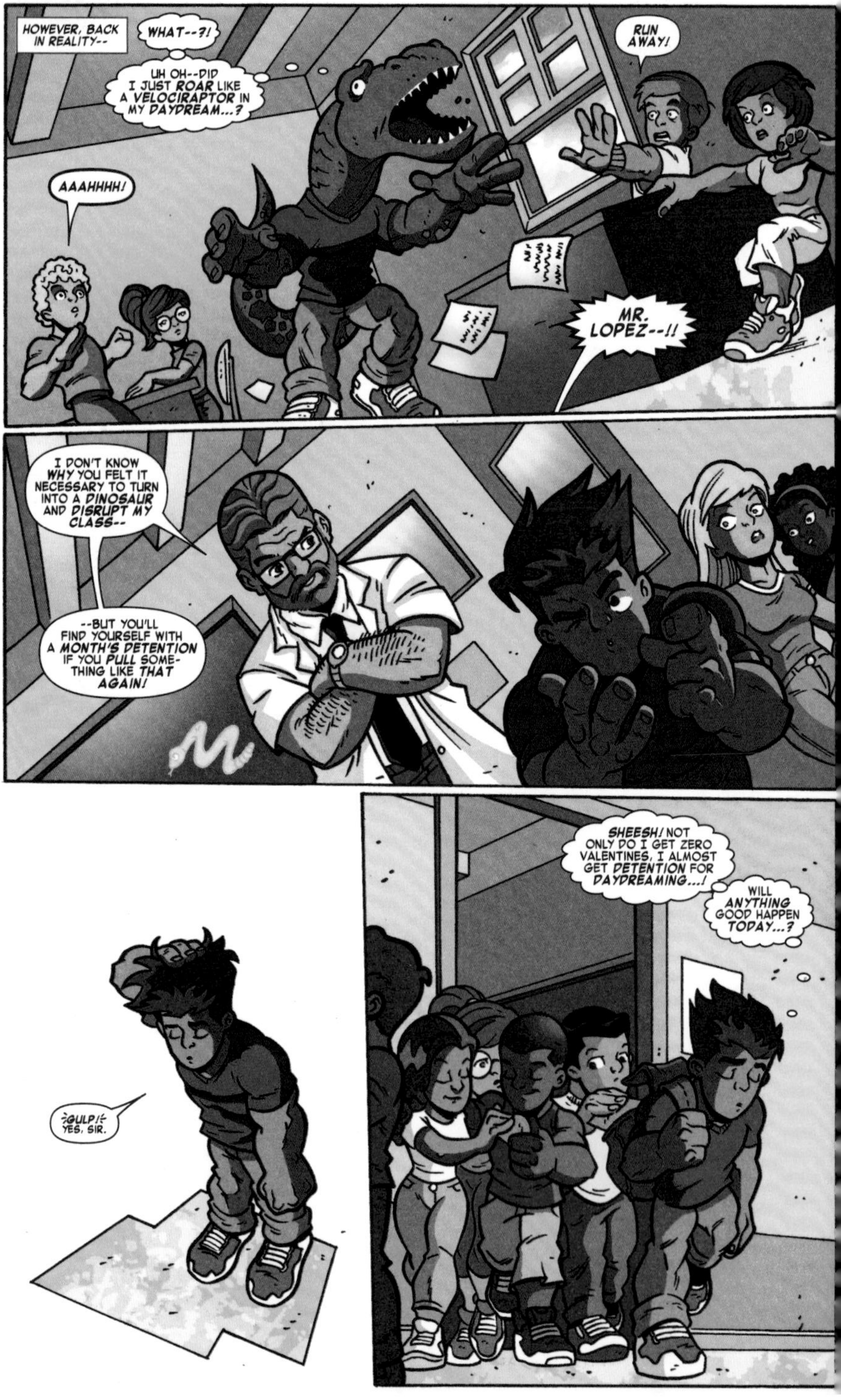
HOWEVER, BACK IN REALITY--
WHAT--?!
UH OH--DID I JUST ROAR LIKE A VELOCIRAPTOR IN MY DAYDREAM...?
RUN AWAY!
AAAHHHH!
MR. LOPEZ--!!
I DON'T KNOW WHY YOU FELT IT NECESSARY TO TURN INTO A DINOSAUR AND DISRUPT MY CLASS--
--BUT YOU'LL FIND YOURSELF WITH A MONTH'S DETENTION IF YOU PULL SOME-THING LIKE THAT AGAIN!
GULP! YES, SIR.
SHEESH! NOT ONLY DO I GET ZERO VALENTINES, I ALMOST GET DETENTION FOR DAYDREAMING...!
WILL ANYTHING GOOD HAPPEN TODAY...?

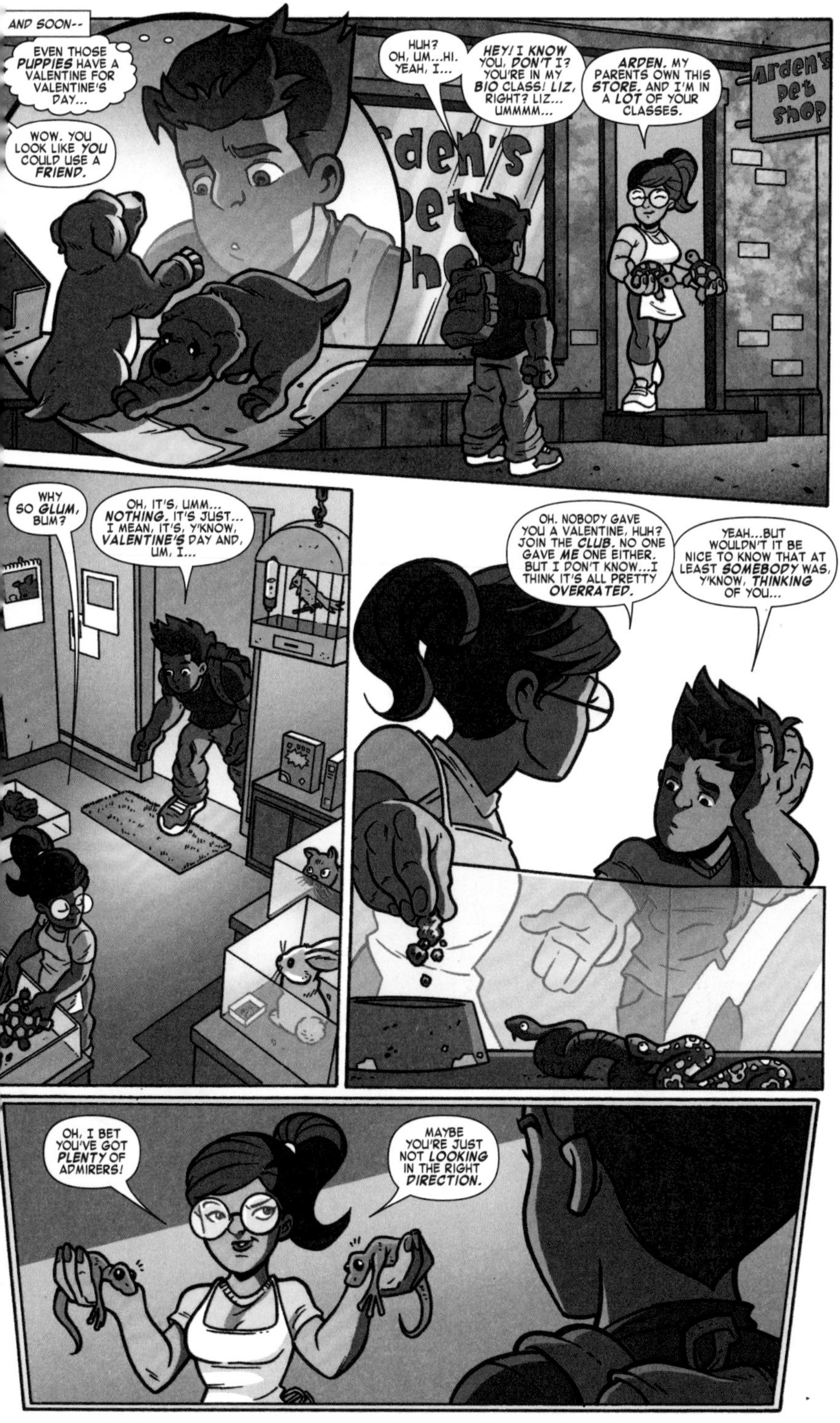
AND SOON--
EVEN THOSE PUPPIES HAVE A VALENTINE FOR VALENTINE'S DAY...
WOW. YOU LOOK LIKE YOU COULD USE A FRIEND.
HUH? OH, UM...HI. YEAH, I...
HEY! I KNOW YOU, DON'T I? YOU'RE IN MY BIO CLASS! LIZ, RIGHT? LIZ... UMMMM...
ARDEN. MY PARENTS OWN THIS STORE. AND I'M IN A LOT OF YOUR CLASSES.
Arden's Pet Shop
WHY SO GLUM, BUM?
OH, IT'S, UMM... NOTHING. IT'S JUST... I MEAN, IT'S, Y'KNOW, VALENTINE'S DAY AND, UM, I...
OH. NOBODY GAVE YOU A VALENTINE, HUH? JOIN THE CLUB. NO ONE GAVE ME ONE EITHER. BUT I DON'T KNOW...I THINK IT'S ALL PRETTY OVERRATED.
YEAH...BUT WOULDN'T IT BE NICE TO KNOW THAT AT LEAST SOMEBODY WAS, Y'KNOW, THINKING OF YOU...
OH, I BET YOU'VE GOT PLENTY OF ADMIRERS!
MAYBE YOU'RE JUST NOT LOOKING IN THE RIGHT DIRECTION.

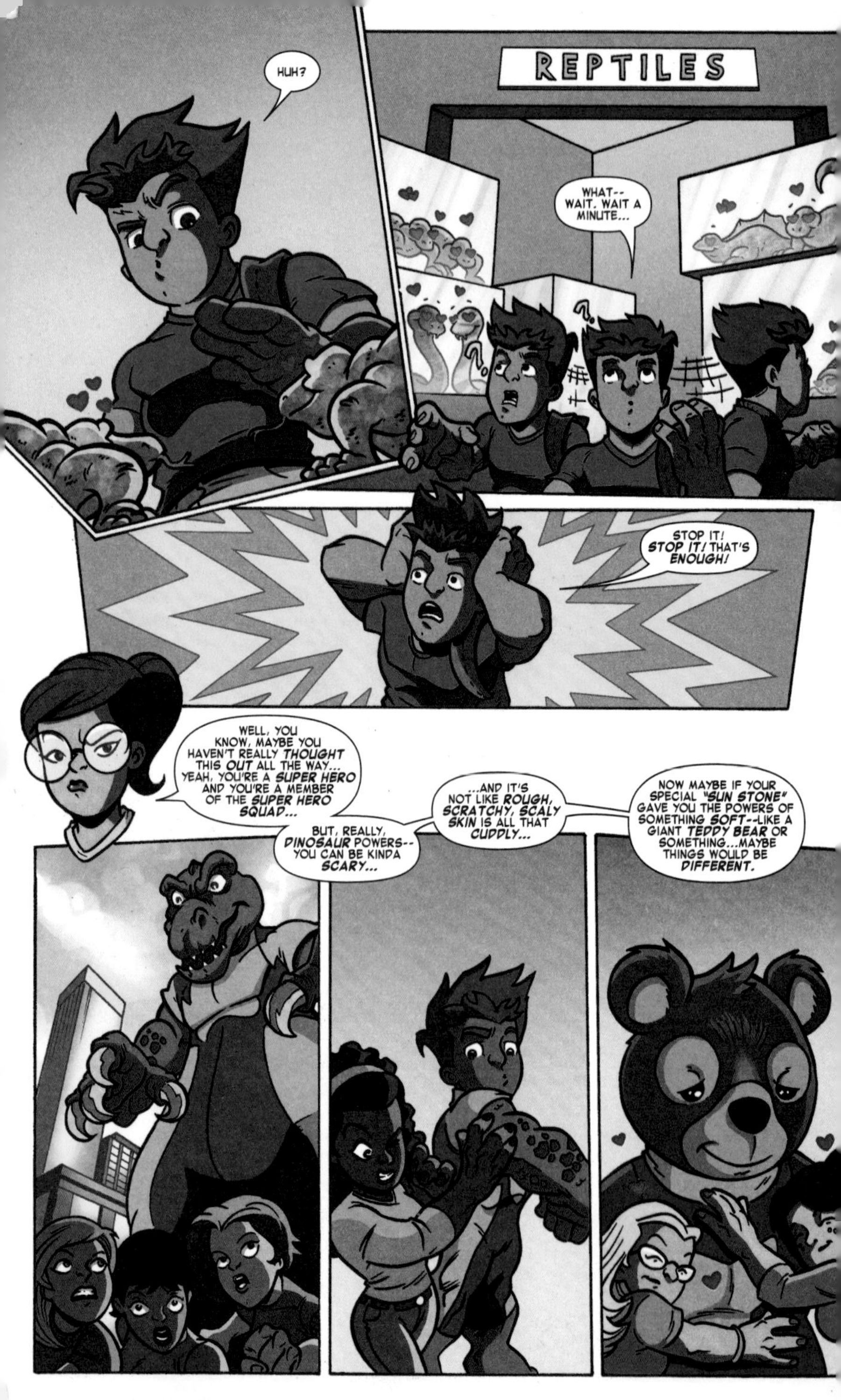
REPTILES
HUH?
WHAT-- WAIT. WAIT A MINUTE...
STOP IT! STOP IT! THAT'S ENOUGH!
WELL, YOU KNOW, MAYBE YOU HAVEN'T REALLY THOUGHT THIS OUT ALL THE WAY... YEAH, YOU'RE A SUPER HERO AND YOU'RE A MEMBER OF THE SUPER HERO SQUAD...
BUT, REALLY, DINOSAUR POWERS-- YOU CAN BE KINDA SCARY...
...AND IT'S NOT LIKE ROUGH, SCRATCHY, SCALY SKIN IS ALL THAT CUDDLY...
NOW MAYBE IF YOUR SPECIAL "SUN STONE" GAVE YOU THE POWERS OF SOMETHING SOFT--LIKE A GIANT TEDDY BEAR OR SOMETHING...MAYBE THINGS WOULD BE DIFFERENT.

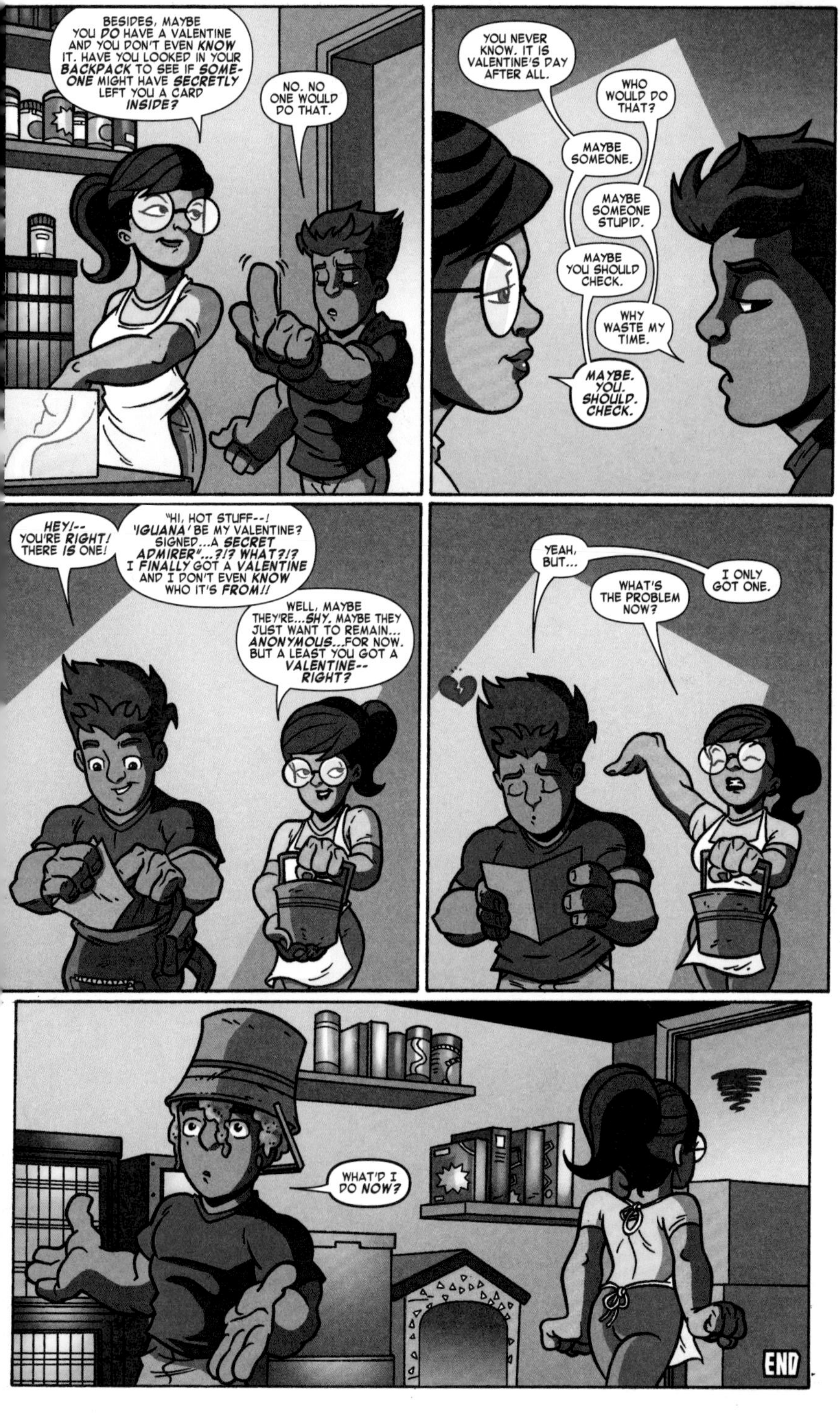

BESIDES, MAYBE YOU *DO* HAVE A VALENTINE AND YOU DON'T EVEN *KNOW* IT. HAVE YOU LOOKED IN YOUR *BACKPACK* TO SEE IF *SOMEONE* MIGHT HAVE *SECRETLY* LEFT YOU A CARD *INSIDE?*
NO. NO ONE WOULD DO THAT.
YOU NEVER KNOW. IT IS VALENTINE'S DAY AFTER ALL.
WHO WOULD DO THAT?
MAYBE SOMEONE.
MAYBE SOMEONE STUPID.
MAYBE YOU SHOULD CHECK.
WHY WASTE MY TIME.
MAYBE. YOU. SHOULD. CHECK.
HEY!-- YOU'RE *RIGHT!* THERE *IS* ONE!
"HI, HOT STUFF--! *'IGUANA'* BE MY VALENTINE? SIGNED...A *SECRET ADMIRER"*...?!? *WHAT?!?* I *FINALLY* GOT A *VALENTINE* AND I DON'T EVEN *KNOW* WHO IT'S *FROM!!*
WELL, MAYBE THEY'RE...*SHY*. MAYBE THEY JUST WANT TO REMAIN... *ANONYMOUS*...FOR NOW. BUT A LEAST YOU GOT A *VALENTINE--RIGHT?*
YEAH, BUT...
I ONLY GOT ONE.
WHAT'S THE PROBLEM NOW?
WHAT'D I DO *NOW?*
END

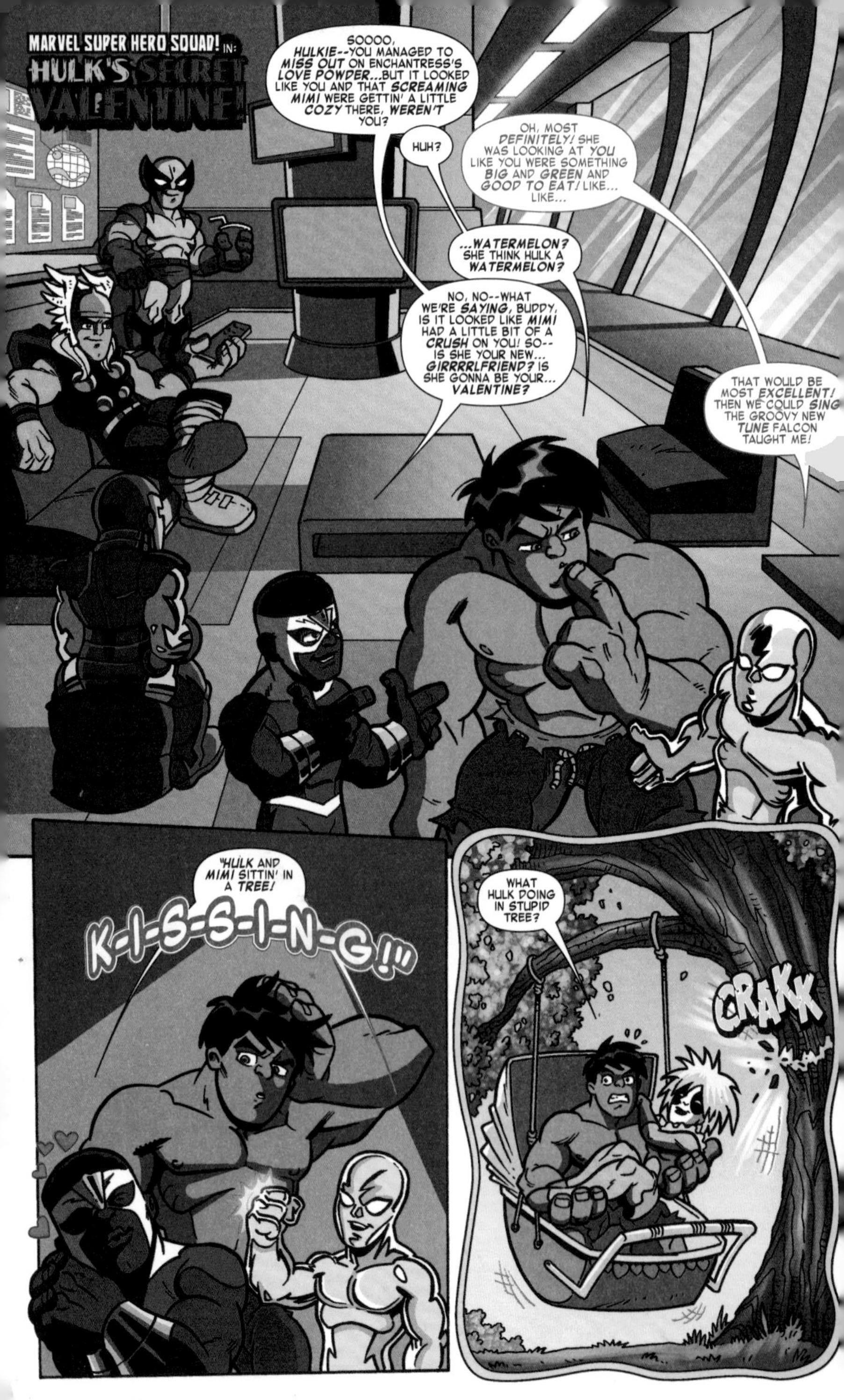
MARVEL SUPER HERO SQUAD! IN: HULK'S SECRET VALENTINE!
SOOOO, HULKIE--YOU MANAGED TO MISS OUT ON ENCHANTRESS'S LOVE POWDER...BUT IT LOOKED LIKE YOU AND THAT SCREAMING MIMI WERE GETTIN' A LITTLE COZY THERE, WEREN'T YOU?
HUH?
OH, MOST DEFINITELY! SHE WAS LOOKING AT YOU LIKE YOU WERE SOMETHING BIG AND GREEN AND GOOD TO EAT! LIKE... LIKE...
...WATERMELON? SHE THINK HULK A WATERMELON?
NO, NO--WHAT WE'RE SAYING, BUDDY, IS IT LOOKED LIKE MIMI HAD A LITTLE BIT OF A CRUSH ON YOU! SO--IS SHE YOUR NEW... GIRRRRLFRIEND? IS SHE GONNA BE YOUR... VALENTINE?
THAT WOULD BE MOST EXCELLENT! THEN WE COULD SING THE GROOVY NEW TUNE FALCON TAUGHT ME!
"HULK AND MIMI SITTIN' IN A TREE!
K-I-S-S-I-N-G!"
WHAT HULK DOING IN STUPID TREE?
CRAKK

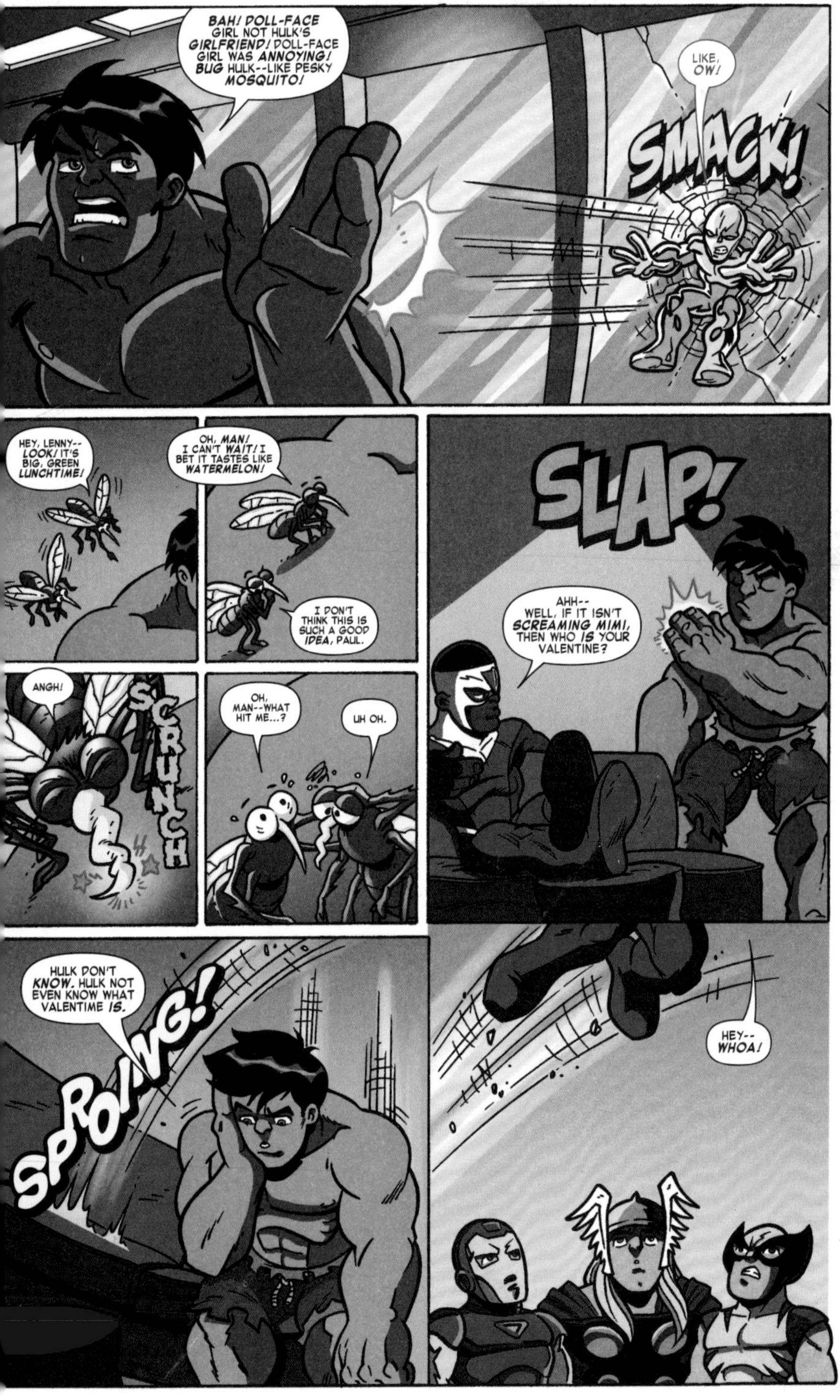
BAH! DOLL-FACE GIRL NOT HULK'S GIRLFRIEND! DOLL-FACE GIRL WAS ANNOYING! BUG HULK--LIKE PESKY MOSQUITO!
LIKE, OW!
SMACK!
HEY, LENNY-- LOOK! IT'S BIG, GREEN LUNCHTIME!
OH, MAN! I CAN'T WAIT! I BET IT TASTES LIKE WATERMELON!
I DON'T THINK THIS IS SUCH A GOOD IDEA, PAUL.
SLAP!
AHH-- WELL, IF IT ISN'T SCREAMING MIMI, THEN WHO IS YOUR VALENTINE?
ANGH!
SCRUNCH
OH, MAN--WHAT HIT ME...?
UH OH.
HULK DON'T KNOW. HULK NOT EVEN KNOW WHAT VALENTIME IS.
SPROING!
HEY-- WHOA!

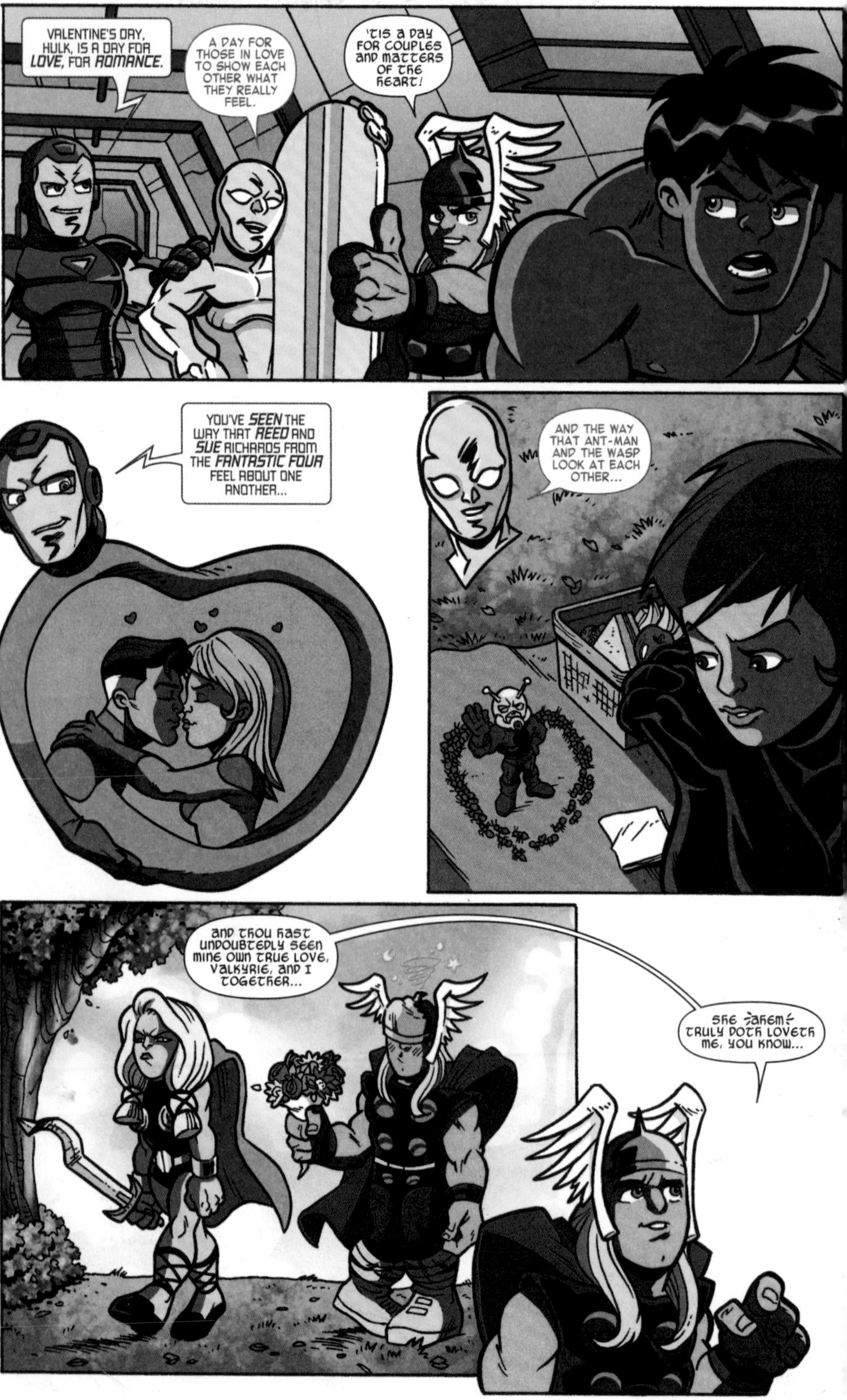
VALENTINE'S DAY, HULK, IS A DAY FOR LOVE, FOR ROMANCE.
A DAY FOR THOSE IN LOVE TO SHOW EACH OTHER WHAT THEY REALLY FEEL.
'TIS A DAY FOR COUPLES AND MATTERS OF THE HEART!
YOU'VE SEEN THE WAY THAT REED AND SUE RICHARDS FROM THE FANTASTIC FOUR FEEL ABOUT ONE ANOTHER...
AND THE WAY THAT ANT-MAN AND THE WASP LOOK AT EACH OTHER...
AND THOU HAST UNDOUBTEDLY SEEN MINE OWN TRUE LOVE, VALKYRIE, AND I TOGETHER...
SHE -AHEM- TRULY DOTH LOVETH ME, YOU KNOW...

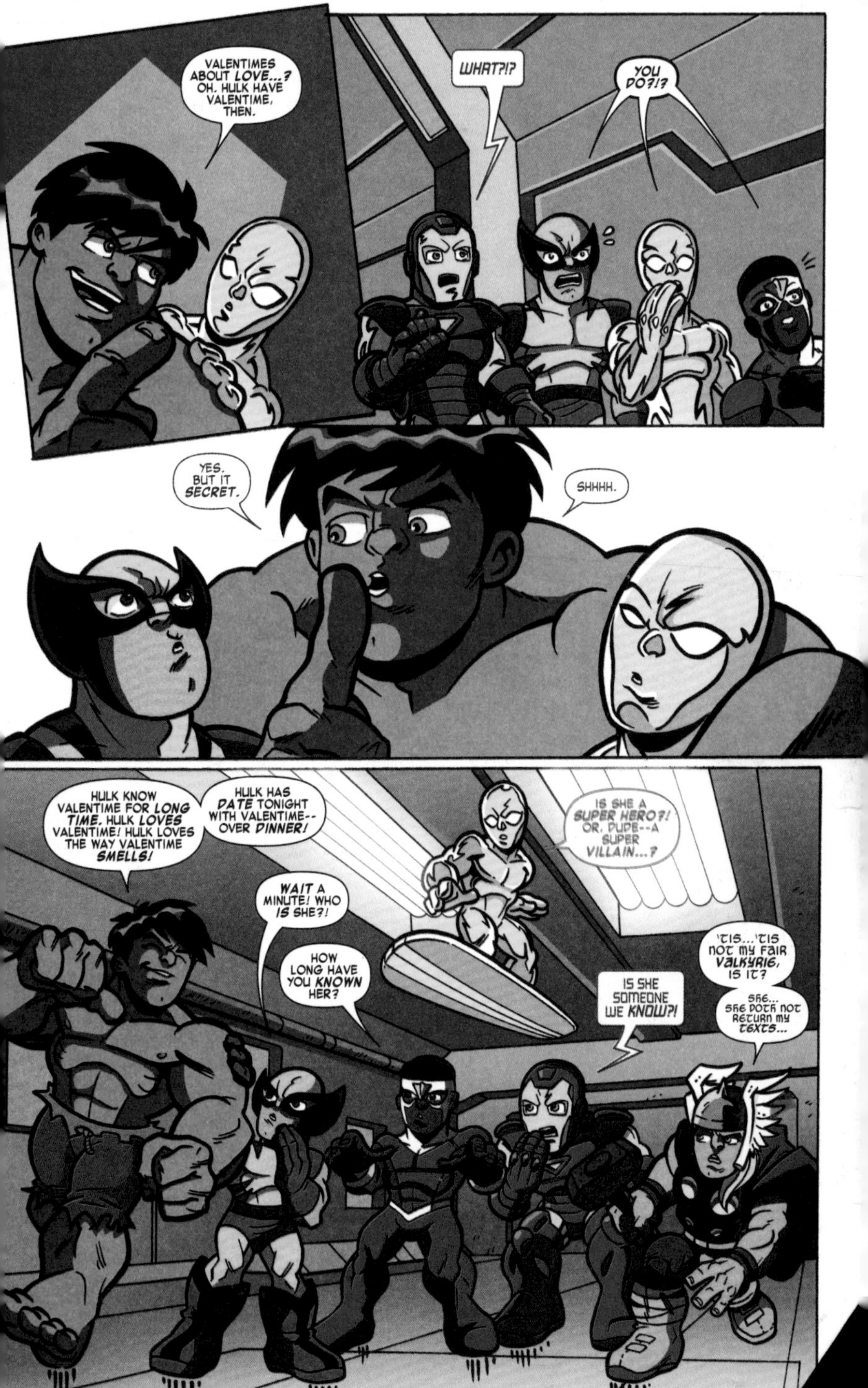
VALENTIMES ABOUT LOVE...? OH. HULK HAVE VALENTIME, THEN.
WHAT?!?
YOU DO?!?
YES. BUT IT SECRET.
SHHHH.
HULK KNOW VALENTIME FOR LONG TIME. HULK LOVES VALENTIME! HULK LOVES THE WAY VALENTIME SMELLS!
HULK HAS DATE TONIGHT WITH VALENTIME-- OVER DINNER!
IS SHE A SUPER HERO?! OR, DUDE--A SUPER VILLAIN...?
WAIT A MINUTE! WHO IS SHE?!
HOW LONG HAVE YOU KNOWN HER?
IS SHE SOMEONE WE KNOW?!
'TIS...'TIS NOT MY FAIR VALKYRIE, IS IT?
SHE... SHE DOTH NOT RETURN MY TEXTS...

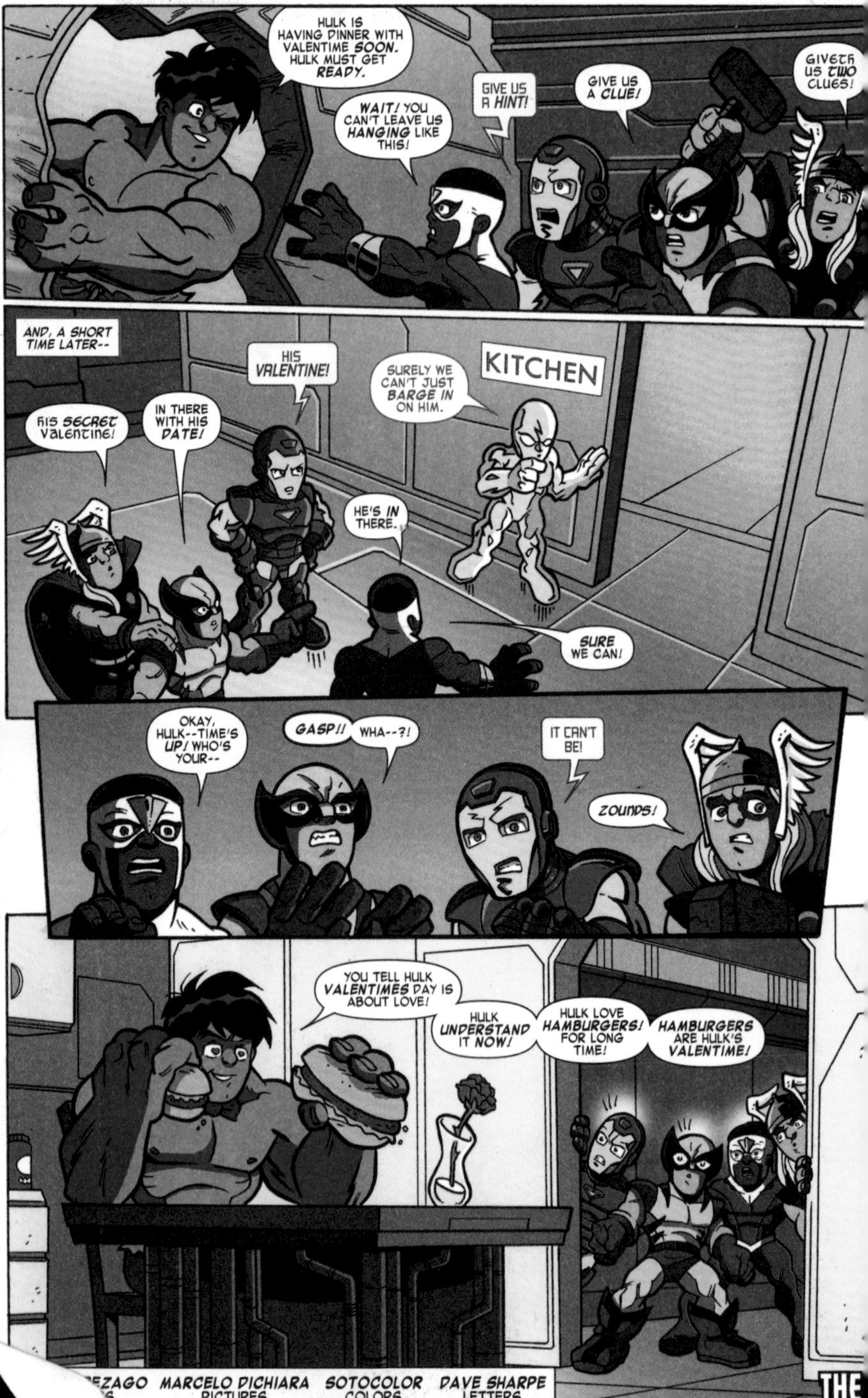
HULK IS HAVING DINNER WITH VALENTIME SOON. HULK MUST GET READY.
WAIT! YOU CAN'T LEAVE US HANGING LIKE THIS!
GIVE US A HINT!
GIVE US A CLUE!
GIVETH US TWO CLUES!
AND, A SHORT TIME LATER--
HIS SECRET VALENTINE!
IN THERE WITH HIS DATE!
HIS VALENTINE!
SURELY WE CAN'T JUST BARGE IN ON HIM.
KITCHEN
HE'S IN THERE.
SURE WE CAN!
OKAY, HULK--TIME'S UP! WHO'S YOUR--
GASP!!
WHA--?!
IT CAN'T BE!
ZOUNDS!
YOU TELL HULK VALENTIMES DAY IS ABOUT LOVE!
HULK UNDERSTAND IT NOW!
HULK LOVE HAMBURGERS! FOR LONG TIME!
HAMBURGERS ARE HULK'S VALENTIME!
EZAGO MARCELO DICHIARA SOTOCOLOR DAVE SHARPE
S PICTURES COLORS LETTERS
ITZ NATE COSBY JOE QUESADA DAN BUCKLEY ALAN FINE
EDITS EDITOR EDITOR-IN-CHIEF PUBLISHER EXECUTIVE PRODUCER
THE END